Influence in the Workplace

▼ Maximizing Personal Empowerment

Dennis Phillips, Ph.D. ▼ **Les Wallace, Ph.D.**

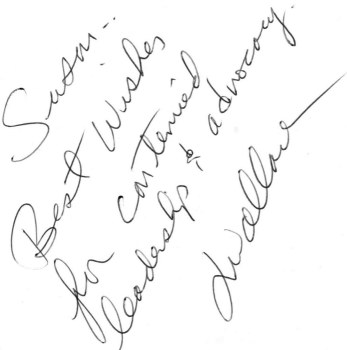

KENDALL/HUNT PUBLISHING COMPANY
2460 Kerper Boulevard   P.O. Box 539   Dubuque, Iowa 52004-0539

Table of Contents

2. Skills and Strategies: The Foundation for Personal Empowerment,   15

3. Developing Functional Maturity,   41

5. *Consultative Phase* Maturity: Advanced Stages of Employee Development, 83

6. Organizational Politics, 101

Foreword

Influence in the Workplace: A Career Building Perspective

If you've been attending to the business press reports of the last few years, you'll recognize these headlines:

"American Productivity Lags, Trade Deficit Grows."

"Burnout Taking Toll on Business Professionals."

"America's Toughest Bosses Extract Extra Effort."

"Progressive Companies Changing The Face of Corporate Culture."

"Financial Justification, Cost Reduction Bring Alternative-Reward Strategies."

"Who Needs a Boss? Not Self Managed Workers."

"Employee Involvement Gets Supporting Compensation System."

"Workforce 2000 Impacting Business Today."

"No More Jobs: Just Skill Sets."

These contemporary messages clearly suggest the future for American workers. "Workforce" is the focus for this decade both here and abroad. Increasing global competition, continued consumer pressure for quality, streamlining of hierarchies and cutbacks in staffing—these emerging characteristics of the 21st century workforce present new challenges and opportunities.

The Dynamic Workplace: Leading Trends

We see several key trends for the next decade:

1. Diversity

A multi-cultural workforce and an improved gender balance in business leadership will require greater sensitivity to other people and other cultures.

2. Lifelong Learning

A more highly educated workforce and greater lifelong learning among adult workers will make the work environment more challenging.

3. Reward Systems

Flexible reward systems will compensate workers based on skills and knowledge and work teams on gain sharing. Workers will choose from a non-traditional buffet of benefits and family support programs.

4. Work Teams

Multifunctional, cross trained, self directed teams will play a greater role in business production and service. The traditional roles of supervisor and employee will be defunct. People will no longer have ''jobs.'' Instead, they will have sets of skills applied to team product or service obligations.

5. Individual Competencies

In view of technological innovation, real time problem solving, and the empowerment of self managing work teams, workers will need to mature their decision making and interpersonal skills.

Employees wanting professional credibility and influence must apply some lessons from the past to these trends. This book focuses on those lessons as they influence (and can be influenced by) nonsupervisory personnel in the American workforce.

Technical vs Interpersonal Competence

During the 1980's, it became generally recognized that interpersonal skills account for about 80% of professional success while technical skills account for only about 20%. This formula is likely to remain a stable guideline for the future. While technical skills remain essential for gaining entre and performing well in organizations, few people dispute the critical importance of interpersonal skills in achieving personal influence. Both the service and manufacturing sectors have recognized the "thinking power" of human resources as a competitive advantage, much as technology was recognized in the last decade.[1] To tap this advantage, top executives are now pressuring managers to learn new interpersonal skills.

Employability and Interpersonal Competence

As global business moves from a manufacturing-dominated economy to a service-intensive economy, the importance of communication skills is magnified. Key theorists recognize that worker security in a changing business climate will mean being "employable." "Employability security rests on the knowledge that competence is growing to meet tomorrow's challenges, that today's work includes the learning and experience to enhance future opportunities—whether with a current employer, with another company, or as an entrepreneur."[2] Whatever the business, the developing trends are clear and the conclusion certain: tomorrow's peak performing workers must be as sophisticated in "people skills" as they are technically proficient.

Mature communication and interpersonal abilities are critical to professional success for these reasons:

▼ With these skills workers can work successfully with the different personalities within their work teams and organizations.

▼ Personal influence upon the work environment increases as skills in promoting and negotiating increase.

▼ Those who have the skills are more frequently sought out for management and leadership positions because of their ability to deal successfully with people.

Though we recognize the value of people skills, we do not intend to suggest that workers lacking in technical skills but good with people will be successful. Indeed, we believe that each individual must achieve and maintain technical competence. However, one of the most neglected areas of professional development in both technical and collegiate programs is personal relations, especially as it involves nonsupervisory employees and staff. This is unfortunate, for deficiency in these skills reduces individual productivity and organizational performance. Also, the basic skills involved are not difficult to learn.

Influence in the Workplace: A Preview

First, we explain how organizations evaluate employee performance and credibility. With this in mind we describe communication skills and strategies that are critical to self development. Chapter one addresses formal organizations and the dimensions of personal and professional competence they usually expect their employees to attain. Chapter two reviews basic communication approaches, skills, and consequences.

Second, with due consideration for the complex dynamics of organizational environments, we identify three phases of development in the nonsupervisory work experience and discuss the skills involved in each. This material is offered to guide personal growth, satisfaction, career enhancement, and the ability to cope with stress. Chapters three, four, and five offer insights and guidelines regarding expectations, responsibilities, and the selection of skills and strategies at different stages in professional maturity. We also develop the means to celebrate achievement and assess additional opportunities.

Finally, in chapter 6, we examine the "politics" and usually unmentioned "realities" that exist in organizational life.

One part of our approach was originally motivated by the work of Paul Hersey and Kenneth Blanchard on situational leadership.[3] They propose a leadership approach that begins with sensitivity to and diagnosis of variables in the workplace—the most critical of which is the work-related maturity of workers. They then present guidelines for managerial behavior that will stimulate productivity. These ideas are further developed in publications such as *Management of Organizational Behavior* and *The One-Minute Manager* series.[4]

In our own work with industry, we found the Hersey/Blanchard foundation helpful in developing core communication skills and strategies for leaders. We have tested these ideas with thousands of people—managers and those whose work they oversee. This has led us to identify specific behaviors associated with levels of maturity in the workplace, to isolate the skills leaders need to facilitate a positive working relationship with employees, and, most significantly, to develop strategies for nonsupervisors to maximize their chances of work success.

Naturally, any presentation of core skills and strategies is open to differences of opinion. As with all human behavior, we are dealing with probabilities and commonly observable tendencies, not certainty. Nevertheless, our approach is based on scholarly theory and research and 40 combined years of professional experience, education, training, and consulting with business and industry. We do not claim to have provided comprehensive coverage of all the issues and skills each reader may feel important. We do know that the skills, strategies, and ideas presented here have been helpful to our clients and students.

DENNIS D. PHILLIPS, Ph.D.
LES WALLACE, Ph.D.

Endnotes Foreword

[1]Joann Lublin, "Trying to Increase Worker Productivity, More Employers Alter Management Style," *Wall Street Journal*, February 13, 1992, p. B1; John Zenger, "Supervisors of the Future," *Small Business Reports*, March, 1991, pp. 16–21; Jan Schilder, "Work Teams Boost Productivity," *Personnel Journal*, February, 1992, pp. 67–71.

[2]Rosabeth Kanter, "Globalization/Localism: A New Resources Agenda," *Harvard Business Review*, March-April, 1991, p. 9.

[3]Paul Hersey and Kenneth H. Blanchard, "Life Cycle Theory of Leadership," *Training and Development Journal*, May, 1969, pp. 26–34.

[4]Paul Hersey and Kenneth H. Blanchard, *Management of Organizational Behavior*. Englewood Cliffs, N.J.: Prentice-Hall, Inc., 1982; Kenneth Blanchard and Spencer Johnson, *The One Minute Manager*. New York: William Morrow and Company, Inc., 1981; Kenneth Blanchard and Robert Lorber, *Putting the One Minute Manager to Work*. New York: William Morrow and Company, Inc., 1984; Kenneth Blanchard, Patricia Zigarmi, and Drea Zigarmi, *Leadership and the One Minute Manger*. New York: William Morrow and Company, Inc., 1985.

Chapter

Organizations and Their Culture

The treatment of employees within the organization is dependent upon the management philosophy of the ownership. That is their prerogative.

Formal Organizations and Expected Outcomes

In profit making organizations, owners and stockholders expect a monetary return on investment as their objective. While they may have other goals, stockholders in profit making businesses evaluate success through financial return on investment. Not-for-profit organizations provide specific community services or pursue environmental, social or educational objectives. Stakeholders in not-for-profit organizations include those benefitting from the activity as well as the organization's funding source (taxpayers, foundation, contributors). They customarily measure success based on social impact or levels of service achieved for constituents.

In either case, the organization takes in resources (raw materials, human resources, money) and manufactures, converts, or organizes them into products or services. Organizations contract with workers to produce the products and services needed to achieve agreed-upon objectives. Goal-directed activity requires that work be structured in a particular way to assure success. By "structure" we mean organization structure, chain of command, and division of labor. A "formal organization," therefore, has four key dimensions: formal objectives, coordinated procedures for accomplishing these, human resources with contracted performance expectations, and an organizational design that defines the authority and coordinating relationships among people.

The Impact of Organizational Structure and Management Philosophy

While organizations need structure to function, organizational structures vary. They may be hierarchical, flat, matrix, centralized, or decentralized. Management philosophy determines how employees are treated. And there are many management styles. In simplistic terms, these range from authoritative to laissez faire.[1] Somewhere in the middle is a philosophy widely referred to as the human relations approach.

Analyzing these management styles provides a worker's primer for developing appropriate behavior within your organization.

Authoritative structures are directive. Decision-making power is concentrated at the top, and responsibility for implementation is distributed downward through many levels of middle management. Nonmanagers have little to say about what happens. Upper-level managers rarely show interest in hearing from people in lower levels. Such structures tend to be relatively tall hierarchies, with many layers between the chief executive officer or president and the ordinary workers. Middle managers in the authoritarian-led organization tend to model the style of the upper echelon managers. They tend to develop the perception (accurate or not) that the top level style is the "right" style.

The autocratic organization has been the class American corporation toward which labor forces initially organized to increase worker rights. Despite the aversion to it expressed by some, especially the more educated people in the work force, the autocratic philosophy results in goal achievement, especially in the short term. There is little argument that it can be successful in terms of speedy decision making and short term productivity. In fact, *Fortune* magazine cautions that this philosophy may become more prevalent as struggling American businesses initiate turnaround strategies: "As global competition heats up and turmoil rocks more industries, tough management should spread. So look for more bosses who are steely, super demanding, unrelenting, sometimes abusive, sometimes unreasonable, impatient, driven, stubborn, and combative."[2]

Laissez-faire organizations, which by definition are non-directive or "hands off," have loose structures and allow extraordinary worker freedom. To the inexperienced eye, such organizations seem to provide wonderful opportunities. However, the lack of structure is frequently, in itself, inhibiting. Administrative officials at Buena Vista College ascribed to such a philosophy when they put together a team of well-educated administrative professionals using loose, undirected supervision and structure. They scrapped the approach shortly after starting, describing the experience as pure chaos.[3] While personal freedom is an important reward to seek, a laissez faire structure does not result in consistent organizational outcomes and is at a disadvantage in a competitive environment. In smaller units of a larger organization, staffed by experienced and self disciplined professionals (e.g. pure research, research and development units, and some "think tanks") a less directive environment may work. However, an organization-wide approach failing to provide some structure, direction, and accountability, either autocratic or participative, is not likely to succeed. It is comparatively rare in America.

Human relations firms place a premium on the development and satisfaction of workers. They see employees as "human resources" to be nurtured and supported. This has everything to do with organizational success. As this philosophy has evolved, however, it has taken on more complex dimensions and applications. Human relations organizations focus not only on worker satisfaction but also on the development of worker competency, self motivation, productivity, and, to a degree, autonomy. Recent studies describe this style as "democratic," "participative" or "collaborative." In these environments self managed work teams give employees more decision-making power.[4] In such organizations concerns for people and organizational achievement are balanced. These organizations are founded on the premise that well informed employees, who are involved in decision making and recognized for performance will produce more and be more creative. Such organizations tend to have fewer layers of middle management and devise systems whereby all employees can innovate and influence organizational change. While major decisions on corporate strategy are still reserved for ownership, day-to-day work decisions are spread to the lowest levels. Although this approach has been around for years, and its successes broadly documented as early as the 1960s by progressive management leaders such as Rensis Likert, it received renewed attention during the 1980's when American businesses struggled to keep pace with consumer demands, reacted to increased global competition and adapted to changing technological and environmental pressures. The "human factor" re-surfaced as critical to needed innovation and change.[5]

Two conclusions are important for the career building employee to note: (1) ownership (stockholders, boards, government officials, top management) has the authority to dictate structural philosophy and performance standards for the organization; (2) different approaches to management can be successful depending upon many variables. As we move toward the year 2000 and beyond, however, the meaning of "success" is likely to be redefined.

Assessing Corporate Culture

Ownership philosophy results in a behavioral system for conducting business, and this system produces a distinct environment for work referred to as "corporate culture."[6] Much management literature discusses corporate or organizational culture in terms of the "values," "traditions," and "symbols" important to the organization. While cultural symbols are important, we prefer to define and evaluate culture by focusing on leadership behaviors: how people are treated and what priorities guide decision making. Therefore, **we use corporate culture to mean the behaviors and beliefs used by an organization to set strategy, develop goals, establish operating systems and daily routine, reward members, and serve customers and stakeholders.**

The employee who wants to develop a platform for empowerment should recognize that corporate culture is best understood by examining six key areas of organizational behavior:

▼ Leadership/Management Styles:

Are decision making and problem solving processes authoritative or participative? Are managers conservative? Or do they take risks? Are they resistant to change or do they welcome it? What happens to employee input? Is a long range vision communicated to employees? How are plans developed?

▼ Communication Flow:

Is communication open (lots of information shared)? Is organizational and task information received in a timely manner? Is information usually clear? Do people in different departments communicate with each other? Is performance feedback provided regularly? Does the organization recognize and use the "internal customer" concept?

▼ Performance Orientation:

Does the organization regularly achieve its goals? Does it have clearly defined outcomes? Is it financially successful? Does it use total quality and continuous improvement systems and tools? Does it recognize accomplishment? Does it assess performance baselines from peer competition? Does it maintain technical proficiency? Is there a sophisticated management information system? Is this available to work teams?

▼ Customer Responsiveness:

Does the company have well defined systems to measure customer satisfaction? Are changes in products and services linked to customer attitudes and needs? Do work teams regularly receive information about customer concerns?

▼ Employee Satisfaction:

Are human resources practices traditional or progressive? Is there a commitment to employee training and development? Is there high turnover or high retention? Are employee opinions surveyed and followed up? Are employees generally proud of their work and their company? Is accomplishment recognized?

▼ Innovation:

Does the business have state of the art services and products? Are employees constantly changing for the good? Does the organization appear comfortable with change? Is there continuous improvement in productivity and quality? Does the organization try new techniques early in their introduction or only after others have used them for awhile?

Answers to such questions will indicate whether the approach to people and their ideas is authoritarian, more focused on "human relations" approaches, or laissez faire. Closed cultures restrict communication flow, display interdepartmental competitiveness rather than collaboration, and criticize rather than coach and train. Decision making is in the hands of management with little or no involvement by employees—even in smaller day-to-day decisions impacting their jobs.

Organizations also vary in their ability to attract and retain top performers. Progressive cultures tend to celebrate innovation and change while more conservative cultures are leery of new ideas and change more slowly. Progressive organizations have clear performance standards, frequently reviewed with employee work groups. More traditional organizations may discuss performance expectations only when a mistake has been made. Open organizations aggressively obtain customer views and share their perceptions, needs, and demands with staff. Progressive organizations facilitate customer and employee contact.

By analyzing organizational culture, new employees can determine the degree of latitude, openness and accountability they have and what behaviors are important and acceptable. In this way they can adapt to job requirements and help the organization while advancing their careers. When accepting a contract, the employee becomes an organizational resource expected to do certain things. At least initially, that means fulfilling performance expectations within an already existing structure and culture. The individual, not the organization, is required to adapt. Employee success, satisfaction, and commitment, therefore, is built first on understanding how the organization operates. Ultimately, success depends upon the degree to which personal goals, values, and skills match the employer's needs.

Throughout this book we focus on the assessments, skills, and strategies that will enable you, as a nonsupervisor, to understand the organizational culture you are in and to take advantage of opportunities to influence the organization. There are two benefits to attaining this empowerment: (1) future employability and career advancement; and (2) more meaningful, less stressful work in the present.

Personal and Professional Credibility

The next logical question is: how do organizations evaluate your progress and potential? As noted, it depends greatly on the overall management philosophy of your employer. But there is one certainty of work life: the greater your credibility, the greater your likelihood of success. We define success as employability, career advancement, satisfaction, and personal influence upon work environment.

Because credibility is so important, whether you are a lathe operator or a physicist, it's important to understand how bosses and organizations evaluate work performance. To a supervisor, performance of assigned tasks and interpersonal skills are measures of a person's contribution to the organization and the degree to which additional opportunity should be granted.

In assessing workers' personal and professional credibility, managers generally focus on three categories of behavior: (1) expertise or competence, (2) believability or trustworthiness, and (3) personableness or dynamism. These categories and resulting conclusions about credibility were first determined in research with public speakers and politicians.[7] And in more than 20 years of consulting work, we have elaborated and validated these principles. Let's consider how these factors apply to your credibility.

Competence

"*Expertise*" or "*competence*" refers to other people's perceptions that you know what you're doing. While this certainly means how you're doing in specific task performance and knowledge, it involves other factors as well. Organized people, who are good problem solvers, who work well in groups, and who are good communicators are perceived as more competent than those with fewer skills in these areas. Therefore, while performance on task is central and critical early on in a job situation, interpersonal skills are also important determinants of credibility.

Trustworthiness

"Believability" or *"trustworthiness"* refers to people's perceptions of your character—that you are honest and dependable. For example, people who are truthful, who do what they say they will do, and who are fair-minded have greater credibility than people who display fewer of these traits. While you may be competent in your job, you must also be trustworthy. Competent but unreliable employees do not have credibility and therefore are customarily given less freedom and opportunity in the workplace.

Personableness

"Personableness," or what the original research labeled as *"dynamism,"* refers to the ease with which people are able to work with you. For example, people who are good listeners, even tempered, cooperative, and appreciative of the contributions of others are considered personable. Significantly, it is impossible to be quite personable while lacking in one of the other two categories and maintain any degree of credibility over the long run. Most people can see through interpersonal "fluff" quickly, especially in the workplace where well rounded performance is important.

To enhance career development and work satisfaction, review the more detailed outline of the factors of personal and professional credibility in the following chart. Pay attention to your strengths and where you need to consider making changes. Realize that others are watching your behavior all the time. Improvement and consistency are important in developing and maintaining your credibility. Also, be honest in assessing your strengths and needs. Successful careers are built upon the firm foundation of mature self-evaluation and commitment to improve.

The Basis of Personal and Professional Credibility

1. *Expertise / Competence*
- ♦ Achieves quality outcomes, knows the job, knowledgeable in field, prepared, always does homework, attends to detail.
- ♦ Adept problem solver, consistently produces results.
- ♦ Respected by staff, manages a well organized area/department.
- ♦ Organized, can organize others.
- ♦ Concise and precise in communication.
- ♦ Balances multiple demands, doesn't over commit, able to prioritize.
- ♦ Good group process leader, summarizes, focuses, leads sequential progress.
- ♦ Identifies additional resources to assist problems (people/information).

2. *Believability / Trustworthiness*
- ♦ Follows up, follows through, keeps word, accountable.
- ♦ Admits mistakes and errors, apologizes when appropriate.
- ♦ Doesn't "play politics" behind closed doors, consistently "fair" with others.
- ♦ Consistent communication style, good listener.
- ♦ Respects diversity of opinion, encourages "hearing" of dissenting opinions, openly discusses pros and cons, withholds judgment until data is in, compromises.
- ♦ Accepts responsibility for "positions" on sensitive issues.
- ♦ Provides rationale behind positions and decisions, openly allows access to information, shares information widely.

3. *Personableness / Dynamism*
- ♦ Good listener, involves others, solicits input from quieter people.
- ♦ Maintains even disposition, sense of humor, laughs at him/herself.
- ♦ Assertive but not aggressive, speaks confidently within/before groups.
- ♦ Works comfortably with diversity of opinion, available, approachable, cooperative.
- ♦ Coaches rather than criticizes, compliments others, sincere praise.

Sources of Power and Implications for Employee Empowerment

Power! Clout! You know people who have it; you want it. What is it? In organizational circles "power" refers to the ability to influence or direct the behavior of others. For example, bosses have authority, through their work performance contract with employees, to organize, direct and control work. That is power. Some of your fellow employees also have power over you. When you are new in a position and need help, co-workers with the needed information have power over you because they have expertise you need to survive. You need to understand different sources of power and how to utilize them in a positive manner for career development.

Basically, there are five types of power in the workplace:[8]

▼ Referent Power

This is the power certain people have because they are admired, liked, and interpersonally competent, and others want to be like them. Such persons become reference points to you, and you allow them to influence you because of your respect and admiration. Others seek to model "referent power."

▼ Expert Power

This is influence based on special knowledge and experience. Experts influence our judgments (have power over us) because we depend upon them for information, insight, or wisdom we lack.

▼ Legitimate Power

This is the power to direct the behavior of others through contract or agreement. Your work contract gives your employer authority to dictate your job standards and compel you to behave in certain ways. You agree to such power, within the law, when you accept employment.

▼ Reward Power

Rewards are behavioral incentives. When you behave a certain way to obtain something you want, you have accepted reward power.

▼ Coercive Power

Punishments and penalties can also direct behavior. Your bank utilizes coercive power to get you to pay your loan on time by its late fee policy. The more you worry about the fee, the greater the bank's influence over your behavior.

The intensity of these various power sources depends upon other variables. For example, the greater the access to other resources such as information, rewards and money, the less may be the influence of some expert or reward power on your behavior. The greater the alternatives (other jobs, for example) the less may be the influence of some legitimate or coercive power. The more employees develop a broad array of work skills and mature in their jobs, the more they can counterbalance the influence of some sources of power.

Which sources of power are of greater interest to career building employees within the workplace? Glance back at the list and notice the order of presentation. Generally, the most significant sources of employee power come from "referent" and "expert" power. Employees have limited access to legitimate or reward power, much less coercive power. However, all employees have equal opportunity to develop as sources of work and team models and to be informed and well versed in workplace issues and strategies; to be seen as "experts," "interpersonally competent," and "admired" co-workers. Everyone has opportunity for power by becoming "high credibility" co-workers or employees.

The reasons why referent and expert power tops the list are simple. Coercive power can only be utilized when one has authority to penalize or punish someone. When access to that authority no longer exists, no power exists. Legitimate power depends upon agreements and contracts, and when they expire or are changed or broken, the power is neutralized. However, information, knowledge, communication skills and interpersonal skills are consistently powerful and influential in the workplace.[9]

How do you build sophisticated referent and expert power? Attend to behaviors typical of high credibility people. Attend to work performance in both task and interpersonal dimensions and develop your career using the guidelines outlined in this book. Recognize that basic communication skills, which retain value in all work settings and human interactions, will increase your power and influence. And when you have opportunity to influence others, do so in a manner that reflects common standards of integrity and ethical behavior; the average person is adept at identifying abuses of power.

Summary

Understanding organizational culture and your expectations within it can lead to positive evaluation and reward in the short term as well as long-term career advancement. The philosophy and skills developed in the next few chapters suggest strategies for developing your credibility at different stages of organizational experience. As a first step, you must meet standards specific to each organization. Having done that, it is how you communicate and behave toward and with other people that extends your credibility and provides additional work and career opportunity.

Endnotes Chapter 1

[1]Early foundations and phraseology regarding structural dimensions of organizations were provided by Kurt Lewin, Ronald Lippitt, and Robert White, "Leader Behavior and Member Reaction in Three 'Social Climates,'" in *Group Dynamics: Research and Theory* (2nd ed.), D. Cartwright and A. Zander, eds. Evanston, IL: Row, Peterson & Company, 1960.

[2]"America's Toughest Bosses," *Fortune,* February 27, 1989, p. 54.

[3]Keith Briscoe, "Colleges, Like Companies, Need Vision to Succeed," *Nation's Business,* December, 1988, p. 12.

[4]See for example: Rosabeth Moss Kanter, *The Changemasters.* New York: Simon and Schuster, 1983; Jack Osburn, *Self Directed Work Teams.* Homewood, IL: Business One Irwin, 1990; Karl Albrecht, *The Creative Corporation.* Homewood, IL: Dow Jones-Irwin, 1987.

[5]See for example: Tom Peters, *Thriving on Chaos,* New York: Knopf, 1987; Michael L. Dertouzos, Richard K. Lester, and Robert M. Solow, *Made in America: Regaining the Productive Edge.* Cambridge, MA: MIT, 1989.

[6]Recent background and elaboration is provided by Charles O'Reilly, "Corporations, Culture, and Commitment: Motivation and Social Control in Organizations," *California Management Review,* Summer, 1989, pp. 9–25; Pamela Shockley-Zalabak and Donald Dean Morley, "Adhering to Organizational Culture; What Does It Mean? Why Does it Matter?" *Group & Organization Studies,* December, 1989, pp. 483–500.

[7]For the antecedents of this current application see: David K. Berlo, J. B. Lemert, and R. J. Mertz, "Dimensions for Evaluating the Acceptability of Message Sources," *Public Opinion Quarterly,* 1969–1970, pp. 563–576.

[8]Peter Blau, *Exchange and Power in Social Life.* New York: John Wiley and Sons, 1964.

[9]For a contemporary validation of these sources of power, see: Allan Cohen and David Bradford, *Influence Without Authority*. New York: John Wiley and Sons, 1990.

Chapter

Skills and Strategies: The Foundation for Personal Empowerment

Because organizational structure is the most important determinant of communication flow, new employees and managers entering organizations are likely to find communication channels well established. While lower level employees may have little control over communication systems, each individual should recognize both the responsibility and opportunity to control his/her communication and behavior. Improving communication skills increases the probability of obtaining the necessary information for job performance,[1] of increasing influence in the organization,[2] and of improving personal satisfaction in work relationships.[3] Interpersonal and communication skills are so important that many organizations hire people in large part based on their communication skills.[4] There is additional evidence that people with more developed communication abilities are promoted more often and reach higher levels in organizations.[5] In the newer models of self directed work teams, team membership selection, leadership, and pay levels all depend significantly upon "social skills competencies."[6]

This chapter focuses on the fundamentals of individual communication skills and strategies. As discussed here, these are skills and strategies for PROACTIVE communication because they require attitudinal and behavioral initiative. Understood properly, these skills require a sensitivity toward both the messages and the people involved in communication situations. Learning and applying these skills and strategies increases the likelihood of communicating effectively and having a greater influence on the outcome of any situation. Effectively sharing and receiving information then becomes a choice and not an accident.

The Role of Supportive Communication Strategies

While there are no guaranteed successes nor failures in any communication situation, people do tend to respond to certain communication efforts in predictable ways. Nearly three decades ago, Jack Gibb identified some of those predictable consequences[7] by outlining a series of communication strategies into continua as presented on the following pages. Communication activity approaching either extreme of a continuum tends to generate the indicated responses. Behavior patterns in either direction result in communication relationships with varying degrees of stress and aggression or openness and trust.

For example, when we use words or a communication style that reflects hostility or lack of concern, we can predict that others will respond defensively. To the extent that we use words or a communication style that display concern and support, we can expect to open channels of communication and develop problem-solving opportunities. Most of us can remember the displeasure or defensiveness we've felt in being around a "know it all" or an extremely critical individual. We can also remember a co-worker or teacher who approached problems and issues more diplomatically and made us feel good about our contributions. Essentially, a communication strategy that allows others the opportunity to be right or feel good about themselves facilitates problem solving, trust, and team building.

Scores of recent articles in both the popular and scholarly literature indicate the value of the supportive approach in management/employee relationships.[8] Why then, doesn't everyone use it? In the work setting there are likely to be many reasons people do not behave more supportively. They may lack skills and understanding. They may have succeeded doing things their own way. They may have little regard for others. They may not be team players. Or the work environment may stress hierarchy rather than team effort. Even among the most well-intentioned people, deadlines and normal work stresses often make control an expedient choice. Everyone should understand that organizations and bosses feel pressures that affect their communication. Nevertheless, we should also understand that "the most important contributor to job satisfaction as an organizational outcome appears to be organizational communication relationships. . . ."[9] Supportive communication contributes significantly to positive working relationships.

While supportive communication increases employee satisfaction, there may be even more important business reasons for learning and applying these principles. Progressive organizations have discovered the competitive value of empowering their workforce. Approaching employees and work teams with supportiveness facilitates innovative thinking, reinforces employee ownership of workplace decisions, and contributes to business success through quality production and service.[10] We will not describe the scholarly underpinnings of "employee involvement" and "participative decision making" as thoroughly as we

Examples of Specific Supportive Communication Behavior[11]

Communication Likely to Arouse Defensiveness and Stress

Evaluation

(Evaluative overtones; personal attack)

"Mary, you can't keep making these simple mistakes."

"Arthur, you caused the accident by ignoring the safety regulations."

Control

(Direct behavior; imposing power; ordering)

"I think my suggestions are fairly clear, Bob, so get back to work"

Neutrality

(Non-caring; clinical; detached)

"That sure sounds like a problem all right."

"I didn't know that."

Superiority

(Emphasizing status, power, intelligence)

"I've worked with this problem for ten years and ought to know what will work."

"I'm being paid to make these decisions, not you."

Certainly

(Knows all the answers; tries to win)

"Of course I'm right."

"I've thought these suggestions through pretty thoroughly so let's not waste time arguing."

Communication Likely to Open Channels and Develop Trust

Description

(Neutral reporting and Observable facts and events)

"We're still having a problem with parts produced."

"This accident appears to involve some differences in interpreting the safety regulations."

Problem-Orientation

(Collaboration; Mutual Inquiry)

"Let's think about the possibilities and get back on this next week"

Empathy

(Caring; respectful; accepting)

"Do you think we ought to do something?"

"I wasn't aware of that; let me make sure I understand."

Equality

(Mutual worth; concern for input and opinion)

"This idea has worked before; do you think it might work in this case?"

"I'll have to make the final decision, but why don't you get your suggestions to me right away."

Provisionalism

(Willing to entertain new ideas; flexible)

"I think I understand, but I'd be interested in your perception."

"I've tried to think these suggestions through pretty thoroughly; can you see anything I may have left out?"

might. But the astute employee will recognize that supportive communication strategies can add value to the individual's career while increasing the financial success of an organization.[12]

Initiating Communication: Responsibilities and Problems

As the initiator of activity and the stimulator of subsequent responses, the person initiating communication must accept responsibility for establishing a positive situation and sending the clearest possible message. Improving sending skills will improve the quality and efficiency of message exchange. In the work environment, the development of sending skills assists employees in overcoming communication barriers.

The origins of poor sending skills include, but are not limited to, these six:

▼ **Lack of skill.** Some people have never learned the basics of effective communication. They may lack control of the language, have had poor role models, or simple lack training.

▼ **Lack of trust.** Some folks do not understand the value of sharing ideas. Others do not wish to share information under the belief it may be used against them. In any organization there may be competition for limited resources. Information can certainly lead to competitive advantage. Many of us have seen others get credit for our ideas.

▼ **Specialization.** "Jargon" has crept into our vocabularies. The speech of doctors, engineers, and mechanics, for instance, is frequently comprehensible only to other doctors, engineers, and mechanics. Specialized vocabulary perpetuates status and tends to inhibit understanding. It can pose an unintended but formidable barrier to communication success.

▼ **Belief that the listener lacks the capacity to understand or doesn't need to understand.** By remaining aloof, the sender isolates him/herself from others who may also need to understand. The barrier to real information exchange is magnified because others begin to imagine hidden meanings from the lack of overt communication.

▼ **Lack of cultural or personal sensitivity.** Not adapting messages to the receiver's cognitive and emotional dictionary interferes with sending success. A speaker may fail to take into account the cultural, gender, or personal factors that cause people to see things differently.

▼ **Apprehension.** Individuals vary in their level of confidence in conversation. While anxiety has many causes, research indicates that, regardless of its origin, apprehension significantly impacts the quality of communication.[13]

These and many other problems affect sending skills, and there are no simple means to solve them. The mastery of language extends beyond specific skill development. Lack of trust or personal confidence may be a problem larger than any specific communication situation. It may even require counseling assistance. However, the communication literature and our own experience as employees, trainers, and consultants suggest several steps that can enhance the probability of communication effectiveness.

Guidelines for Sending Clear Messages

Applied to organizational situations, the following steps provide you with alternatives. They are "proactive" in that they require you to take the initiative for getting the message across. When used consistently, they will improve the quality of information flow and ultimately aid in developing trust, teamwork and individual leadership potential.

▼ **Account for perspective.** Be sensitive to people and their differing frames of reference. Many people are simply not aware of the entire process of communication. Nor do they really think about the people with whom they are interacting. A firm understanding of the communication process including the role of the sender and listener and the importance of the message is the first step in improving communication.

Sensitivity also involves supportiveness. You should want to share information. You should be aware of the range of potential responses. You should assume 100% of the responsibility for getting the message across. This means you need to understand the communication process.

▼ **Assume responsibility.** Think before talking. Whether conversing with a single individual or making a presentation to a larger audience, remember that your listeners will determine how effective you are in sharing ideas. Thinking before you talk and while you talk involves selecting language, concepts, and examples and relevant ideas within the audience's experience.

Do you remember your parent's "count to 10" rule before reacting to a hostile or offensive act? Thinking before talking works similarly. It provides a moment of mental collection before saying something that should not have been said. For at least an instant even after hearing an aggressive comment, organize what you want to say—thus, responding instead of reacting; relating instead of attacking. This is difficult because other people often react and fail to consider the impact of their message before they talk. This is especially true in situations of disagreement and defensiveness. Nevertheless, in communication, there is at least one person with control over words and behaviors: you, the sender. Use cooperative language and tone. In the spirit of Jack Gibb, strive for descriptive, empathic words and meanings, rather than making judgmental statements. In many instances, your self control will set the tone for others, and tempers will be regulated and problems solved.

▼ **Be specific.** Refrain from the use of abstract words or general statements. Use examples and other forms of specific evidence to illustrate and support your ideas. One regular pitfall is the use of the word they. "They won't let me do my job." "They expect too much of me." Listeners wonder: "Who is they? And why won't they let you do your job?" Specificity helps prevent inappropriate interpretations of what you say from forming. It may mean not speaking sometimes, but that is not all bad. Not speaking gives you the opportunity to listen.

▼ **Focus, summarize, and restate.** Do not assume the other person has understood because of a nod of a head or lack of questions. It is helpful to rephrase, perhaps to the point of asking the other person to restate the position: "What did you understand me to say?" The effect of this is to give the other person the opportunity to listen more attentively. A restatement may also bring questions that will clarify the situation.

▼ **Watch for nonverbal responses.** Facial expressions, eye contact, and other nonverbal responses are all clues to understanding. While nonverbal behavior can be ambiguous without clarification, good communicators will be aware of it as a cue for providing restatements and examples, for soliciting questions or comments, or for making sender statements brief. Recognition of nonverbal responses helps others want to listen and want to talk as you show an awareness of their response.

▼ **Utilize multiple modes.** Use a combination of communication channels. In those critical situations, especially related to personal achievement, need, or problems, a written accompaniment or followup to a discussion may be important in reinforcing, clarifying, and documenting what transpired.

It does not matter whether the above steps are applied in conversation with supervisors, peers, subordinates, spouses, judges, or parents; in one-to-one situations, group discussions, or public presentations. Good sending skills promote understanding and encourage positive responses from others. They also encourage others to follow your example.

Effective Listening: Responsibilities and Problems

For an employee, listening skills may be more critical than sending skills. While some research suggests that the most important attribute of an effective supervisor is the ability to listen,[14] for the non supervisor effective listening is an investment in performance.[15] Effective listening helps one learn organizational culture, the formal and informal norms of the organization, and the job expectations. A good listener may be given an important communicative role within the organization.

Although the listener determines the effectiveness of the speaker, the listener is not absolved of responsibility in the information exchange. Often, we hear people say: "I can't understand anything he has to say." Or, "How does she expect me to do the job? She doesn't tell me what to do?" The implication is that the speaker is entirely to blame. Do we expect others to get all the glory and our paychecks as well? Hardly. Therefore, it is essential that we accept responsibility when receiving information. We challenge listeners to be active and assume 100% of the responsibility for getting the message. If the speakers accept a similar responsibility, an understanding should be relatively easy to reach.

Let's first clarify what is meant by active listening. In contrast to hearing—a physiological function of sound entering the ear and being transmitted to the brain—**listening is the act of selecting from, and attaching meaning to, those sounds (and accompanying nonverbal cues).** Listening is a higher cognitive process than hearing. Active listening means accepting personal responsibility for clarifying and understanding messages.

Most experts recognize two categories of listening: deliberative and empathic.[16] Deliberative listening is the ability to hear and clarify information, analyze it, recall it at a later time, and draw conclusions from it. Essentially, it means being able to understand and recall information for later use.

Empathic listening occurs when the receiver recognizes the feelings of the sender. The empathic listener not only understands the information being shared, but also senses underlying emotions of frustration, disbelief, and concern. Empathic listening involves hearing, understanding, and trust. Empathic listeners tend to be better problem solvers, mediators, and opinion leaders.[17]

For any employee, the most important benefit of improved listening is fewer mistakes and misunderstandings. But better listening will also produce a positive atmosphere and improve work relationships.

Many people who believe they are excellent listeners are actually not. Some lack effectiveness because they are not aware of the listening process; they lack awareness of the many techniques involved and do not work at improving. We find that listening problems often arise inadvertently in communication situations, not because people do not want to listen, but rather because they do not work at listening.

Here are five mindsets that diminish listening effectiveness:

▼ **Lazy listening.** Many people respond only to ideas they immediately recognize. They do not try to find importance or interest in other matters. They tune out to new ideas.

▼ **Preconceived attitudes.** Because some people stereotype looks, dress, speech (accents and impediments included), national origin, or position they make judgments without even hearing all or any of what others have to say. They do not work to overcome stereotypes and focus on ideas.

▼ **Preoccupation.** Other things may be pressing on listeners' minds. People preoccupied with solving an unrelated problem or accomplishing a task, for instance, may find information from someone as an infringement on their time and energy.

▼ **Loaded words.** Occasionally, speakers use words or references that are offensive, threatening or critical. Instead of continuing to listen, there is a tendency to react internally and emotionally to the offense.

▼ **Anxiety or fear.** Performance evaluation, whether it be the formal appraisal or a casual evaluation, can arouse anxiety in the receiver, especially if negative. The tendency is to react to the evaluation and miss details and perhaps the total message. Just the sight of a supervisor or advocate can sometimes have the same effect.

This list is not all inclusive. Indeed, if challenged, nearly everyone could come up with long lists of other problems that negatively affect their listening abilities. The important question here is how to overcome the problems.

Guidelines for Effective Listening

We assume you want to listen effectively. If you do, we offer *seven suggestion*s for improvement:

▼ **Stop talking.** It is difficult to receive information from others when attempting to send it yourself. Pausing silently will give you a moment to reflect on what's being said and help you show sensitivity to the sender. If you want to listen, then demonstrate it by being quiet.

▼ **Paraphrase.** Too often people react to bits of communication or unclear communication without taking time to confirm the intended meaning. Paraphrasing is an active attempt to confirm and understand. Because a paraphrase is a descriptive nondefensive response, it also supports empathic listening by giving the other person opportunity to clarify or elaborate without feeling that they have been "attacked." You can introduce a paraphrase in a neutral way: "What I hear you saying is. . . ." "Do you mean . . . ?" "Let me see if I'm understanding you correctly."

Carl Rogers and Richard Farson offer this challenge to people involved in heated exchanges: "Before either participant in the discussion can make a point or express an opinion of his own, he must first restate aloud the previous point or position of the other person. This restatement must be accurate enough to satisfy the speaker before the listener can be allowed to speak for himself."[18] Having tried this in workshops and negotiations, we know you will find it a valuable technique.

▼ **Withhold evaluation.** Whether listening for factual understanding and recall or for emotional content, it is important to withhold evaluation until after you understand. This is difficult. It requires patience. Many people have learned to judge based upon first impressions, looks, and nonverbal cues before considering the message. The mind is like a parachute: it does you no good unless it's open. Your open mind is key to understanding, and a

One of our favorite listening success stories came out of a series of workshops with a national manufacturing company. During the "Effective Listening" portion, an employee asked what to do when his boss verbally admonished him. He explained that his boss seemed to take out frustrations by "yelling" and "name calling" at employees often without reason. We suggested that he try the paraphrase as follows: "Let me see if I understand what you are saying. You believe that I am an (expletive deleted). What I do not understand is the reason for my being an (expletive deleted)."

The employee returned to the following week's workshop, and told the entire group that he tried the suggestion in his best supportive (not patronizing) tone of voice. He said his supervisor was so dumbfounded by the paraphrase and clarification that they both broke out laughing. He vowed to use the paraphrase technique in hostile situations in the future.

positive desire to listen effectively requires that you withhold judgment, at least until after you have confirmed that you understand what is being said.

Perhaps the hardest part of listening is reviewing and mentally summarizing the points that the speaker is making—while suspending judgment. However, combined with the paraphrase, withholding evaluation and projecting positive listening energy allow you to focus on ideas. Once ideas are understood, some degree of evaluation is appropriate. But, you should evaluate ideas not speakers.

▼ **Take notes.** Depending upon the situation, this is not always possible. However, where it is appropriate you should not hesitate to do so. When taking notes, focus on key words and ideas. Be brief. Most often facts are not as crucial in the immediate situation as a grasp of ideas.

▼ **Ask for specifics and/or clarification.** Sound familiar? Even though we know that clarification and specifics are important in sending, many people forget or simply do not provide specifics when sending. As an effective listener, you must take the initiative to get those specifics. It is not appropriate to assume nor is it appropriate to guess, even though many people do so with the weak excuse that they are afraid to ask—afraid that asking would make them look uninformed or inferior. Failing to understand and making mistakes as a result are what make people look inferior. Ask for specifics.

▼ **Watch for nonverbal cues.** Look for behavioral clues that may indicate lack of interest, confusion, mistrust, defensiveness, or fear. Lack of eye contact, fidgeting, a raised voice, frowns—all may signal an important reaction you need to consider or clarify. One communication expert argues that there is intense meaning involved in nonverbal cues.[19] The effective listener is constantly sensitive to nonverbal messages, ready to ask for clarification and to paraphrase to insure that the interpretation of the nonverbal cues is correct.

▼ **Review and summarize.** Consider the complexity of the information and the risk of getting it wrong in determining when to review. For instance, following an orientation session, you may wish to ask what you were supposed to learn. At the end of any session with the supervisor explaining job duties and responsibilities, review what you understood him/her to say. At the end of a departmental meeting, you may need to review what is expected of you.

In one of our research projects,[20] we observed many meetings between a communication executive and others to review progress on various projects. The meetings were useful for all involved. It was amazing, however, how many participants came back to the executive's office (often rather sheepishly) within the hours following the meeting, to clarify what they were supposed to do. While the followup and clarification were well advised, much time and energy was wasted (as well as faces reddened) simply because the review and summary had not taken place at the close of the meeting.

The intent of developing sending and receiving skills is to achieve understanding and improve working relationships. While total understanding may not be possible, a sender willing to accept 100% of the responsibility for the result and a receiver doing the same can improve their chances of reaching an understanding.

Shared Leadership Responsibility: Group Communication Roles

Basic sending and listening skills, applied in supportive one–on-one conversations, give beginning workers concrete advantages. However, as work competence increases and performance recognition is forthcoming, employees may be required to work in more complicated interpersonal situations.[21] They may become involved in group decision making and problem solving. So they will need to communicate in a team environment. And occasionally their work group will want to influence upper-level managers. This places additional pressure on all participants to communicate clearly and persuasively.[22]

As global business management matures, workers are being called on more frequently to participate in group decision making, group problem solving and group planning and evaluation. Whether it be "employee involvement" programs, "self managed work teams" or simply department meetings, most workers will feel the stress of such activities sometime during their career development. The greater the need to achieve and be recognized, the greater the need to understand and utilize group communication skills and strategies that contribute to quality outcomes.

Group leadership is frequently misunderstood. The prevailing attitude on the work floor is that the supervisor, foreman or team leader is responsible for leadership in group decision making and problem solving. The reality is, these folks may be responsible for facilitating discussion and leading the agenda, but all participants share responsibility for the quality of the discussion. Many observers regard leadership as a "collection of roles and behaviors that can be split apart, shared, rotated, and used sequentially or concomitantly. . . ."[23] At any given time, multiple leaders can and do exist in a team.[24]

Shared or "distributed" leadership means that even though a chairperson (supervisor/team leader) may direct the meeting agenda, all group members help direct the discussion. Leadership direction is needed in work on both task and interpersonal relations. Task leadership requires communication that moves the group forward toward accomplishing group duties and objectives. Maintenance leadership involves communication behaviors that smooth interpersonal relations and maintain a supportive and open discussion environment. As you work in teams, you should begin to identify and use the strategies with which you feel most comfortable.

Group Task Leadership Roles

✔ **Initiating:** Activities focused on getting the group started, keeping progress moving and keeping discussion focused.

Examples:
"We're getting off the track."
"We don't seem to have a clear definition of the problem."
"What is our objective?"

✔ **Clarification and Elaboration:** Activities that aid understanding and focus; adding needed information or examples; helping team members better identify issues and ideas.

Examples:
"I'm not sure I understand. Could you give me an example?"
"Do you mean _____ ?" "Are you saying _____".
(paraphrasing)
"Is this a good example of what we're trying to get at?"
"I don't understand why this information is important."

✔ **Information Exchange:** Statements that assist the group in uncovering and sharing information and member opinions.

Examples:
"Does anyone have any more information on this issue?"
"Here's some information I got from the government office."
"What do you think about that idea?" (seeking opinion)
"Here's something that bothers me about that idea." (giving opinion)

✔ **Summarizing:** Statements that synthesize and review what has been discussed or decided; and what might be left to accomplish.

Examples:
"I'm feeling a little lost. Could someone try to summarize for me?"
"Here's where I think we are so far."
"Let's review what we've decided."
"Is this where we ought to go from here?"

✔ **Consensus Taking:** Statements that help the group come to a conclusion.

Examples:

"It looks like most of us feel this idea is probably the best."
"What do the rest of you feel we ought to do?"
"Is there any way we can combine these suggestions?"
"It looks like we have narrowed it to two options."

Group Maintenance Leadership Roles

✔ **Gatekeeping:** Communication designed to assist fair participation by all and to limit interruptions.

Examples:

"Robert, we've heard a lot from you. Can we hear from some of the others?"
"Jennifer, what ideas do you have?"
"Could we take another fifteen minutes to wrap this up before we break?"
"Joe, why don't we let Mary finish before we hear from you?"

✔ **Encouraging:** Statements that reinforce the participation and ideas of others.

Examples:

• Eye contact and attentive listening behavior
"John, that sounds like a good idea."
"I think Margaret had a good point earlier."
"Charlie, I understand what you mean, and it's a point we'll have to consider."

✔ **Harmonizing:** Communication behavior to relieve tension and reduce group friction

Examples:

• Humor.
• Stepping in to point out similarities between opposing ideas.
• Suggesting compromise when differences appear unresolvable.
• Respecting the ideas of all members through polite and courteous communication.

Managing Conflict

Few employees become effective workplace leaders without learning how to deal diplomatically and capably with differences of opinion. The contemporary management emphasis on employee involvement and quality focused task teams guarantees that conflicting ideas and opinions will surface in work groups. Conflict management requires sensitivity, tact, and courage. While sophisticated conflict management training is beyond the scope of this text, you might test your current attitudes and skills by completing our short "Conflict Management Assessment," on the next page. Then return to interpret your responses in view of communication strategies that follow.

Communication Strategies for Managing Conflict

Now interpret your understanding of conflict and communication skills by reviewing the following guidelines. (Suggestions 1–16 correspond to numbers of the "Interpersonal Audit: Conflict Management Competencies")

1. Disagreement promotes creativity by generating a larger pool of ideas and perspective. Members of effective groups are not afraid of diversity of opinion and disagreement. They can manage it. Your ability to be patient with other points of view and to work to understand them will increase your leadership potential. Remember, maintaining openness to other points of view, being a good listener and remaining objective enhances your personal credibility.

2. Conflict management requires keeping disagreement at the idea level rather than the emotional or personal level. Focus on facts rather than personalities, prejudices or uniformed opinions. Recognizing that everybody has a piece of the truth will help the group concentrate on ideas. Try to ignore personal criticisms or emotional language. Think about the facts in the situation. Don't overreact. In a "total quality" environment this "problem" vs. "emotion" focus is enhanced by using "data based" problem solving where the application of statistical tools and graphs is of considerable help.

3. Resolution of conflict (complete and total agreement by all parties) is difficult to attain. People should not expect it. Managing conflict means being fair-minded and keeping the discussion focused on

Interpersonal Audit: Conflict Management Competencies

	Rarely				Often
1. I encourage other points of view because it enhances the creativity of our final product.	O	O	O	O	O
2. I can see the difference between disagreement over issues and disagreement that involves personality.	O	O	O	O	O
3. I believe managing conflicts is more important than resolving conflicts.	O	O	O	O	O
4. I sometimes find myself in conflicts where the final outcome doesn't warrant lengthy discussion & debate.	O	O	O	O	O
5. When I disagree with someone, I sometimes delay in saying so.	O	O	O	O	O
6. When discussing topics with potential for conflict, I break issues down into small parts for discussion.	O	O	O	O	O
7. I find myself saying "I think" a lot.	O	O	O	O	O
8. When I argue with others, I frequently re-state what they say to check my understanding of their position.	O	O	O	O	O
9. I use many examples when arguing a point with others.	O	O	O	O	O
10. When I disagree with someone I closely examine those areas of the problem that we agree upon.	O	O	O	O	O
11. At the end of some meetings I find some people still have different perceptions of the problem or goal.	O	O	O	O	O
12. When I have a frustration or pet peeve that's making me feel hostile, I always explain it to the other person.	O	O	O	O	O
13. When arguing with others I threaten and bluff.	O	O	O	O	O
14. When someone makes a valid point, I frequently tell them they're right.	O	O	O	O	O
15. I believe someone ultimately wins and someone else ultimately loses an argument.	O	O	O	O	O
16. I find conflict ends when the other party says "O.K., you're right, let's do it your way."	O	O	O	O	O

ideas and facts. Workable solutions or agreements don't require everybody to totally agree. "Consensus" does not require everyone to agree 100%, but instead to agree enough that the group can move forward without major resistance.

4. Much personal conflict is about issues that we don't care that much about in the first place. Choose your fights wisely. Don't argue about minor points. J. M. Juran, one of the fathers of "Total Quality Management" reminds us to focus our energies on the "vital fews" vs. the "trivial many" issues confronting us.[25]

5. Express your disagreement right away. Withholding your concerns and springing them on someone later may cause you to be viewed with suspicion. After you have clearly listened to and understood the position, use diplomatic approaches such as "I'm not certain I understand," "I'm not certain I can agree with that without more information," "I have a different view/interpretation of that," or, "I need to think about that for a while." Diplomacy keeps the options open to change your mind, while not directly attacking the other position.

6. Try to break problems down into their component parts. This will help others find common ground and focus on specifics rather than generalities. Diagramming or graphically representing a problem can help people visualize solutions.

7. Offer your ideas as suggestions rather than certainties. Avoid "I think" statements. Instead, use statements like "How does this sound?" "Would this be a possible solution?" Would it help to look at it from this perspective?" Such cooperative approaches reduce defensiveness and create a climate in which differences of opinion are seen as healthy, not damaging.

8. In any conflict situation, a significant portion of the disagreement may be caused by "misinterpretation" of what the other person(s) is trying to say. Paraphrase the ideas and opinions of others to assure you understand. The paraphrase is introduced by such phrases as "Are you saying. . . ." "Do you mean. . . ." "Let me see if I'm understanding you correctly." Help other parties who may be misinterpreting one another by stepping in to clarify and paraphrase.

9. Manage conflict by reducing the level of abstract talk. Be specific. Offer examples or ask for examples to help clarify meaning.

Generalities are susceptible to misinterpretation and lead to unneeded perceptions of disagreement.

10. Try to discover what you do agree on and work from there. Identifying commonality builds a more positive discussion where the objective is clearly to reach a good decision rather than emphasize differences. There are few conflict situations where participants can't find some common ground as a starting point.

11. Always begin meetings with a clear statement of the problem or objective. Too many conflicts stem from different problems or different perceptions of the problem. Make sure from the outset that you're talking about the same issue or concern. In a "total quality" environment, this is accomplished by relying on observation, data gathering and statistical tools and graphs.

12. Openness helps. Share your frustrations diplomatically. Keeping a chip on your shoulder only assures that you will be more emotional. However, own your own emotions rather than blaming them on someone else.

13. Threats or bluffs have no place in problem solving or decision making. Ever! Most people can see through a bluff, and threats only create defensiveness.

14. Be supportive when you can. By acknowledging a good point or idea made by another person, you show that you're objective and a good sport. This improves teamwork.

15. Adopt a win-win orientation. Conflicts do not have to be win-lose battles. Groups can discuss, compromise or see new ideas that allow all members to feel they have made valuable contributions. Your purpose is not to make others feel their ideas or positions are worthless. When a final decision is reached (or arbitrated) remind everyone involved how the discussion helped clarify the issues. All input is helpful, and everyone shares in the final outcome.

16. Don't assume conflict is over until you've checked your perception with the other parties. While not everyone may be ecstatic over the decision, you do need to confirm that they will not resist moving on from here.

Assessing Your Communication Development Needs

All organizations have "customers" with whom they must communicate effectively. During the 1980's, recognition of this fact produced a frenzy of customer relations books, workshops, and corporate programs. However, a "customer relations" focus is needed within an organization as well. If employees are not directly serving the organization's customers, they should serve someone who is. Organizational leaders now recognize the value of "service" and "support" relationships among departments. Self managed work teams and interdisciplinary task forces need to help each other.

Whether you have direct contact with customers external to your organization or simply must apply customer relations to your interpersonal and interdepartmental relationships, consider adopting a "service" perspective.

Internal and External Customer Relations Skills: The C.P.R.™ Model.

Three categories of communication and problem solving skills are most critical to achieving service excellence. These may more easily be remembered and evaluated using a "C.P.R." model.[26]

"C" Communicate with Courtesy

Customers should perceive your style as consistent with common courtesy. You should always be attentive and well mannered. Whatever the level of problem, concern, frustration or information sharing, you should be personable, supportive and responsive. Use the following questions to evaluate yourself in this regard:

▼ Do you respond promptly to customer inquiry or request? Do you smile, introduce yourself if necessary, use "please" and "thank you" when conducting business? Do you maintain eye contact and a respectful tone or voice?

▼ Do you use standard telephone courtesy?

▼ Do you maintain a quiet environment? Are you careful of overheard conversations? Do you protect confidentiality when discussing customers' needs?

▼ Are you attentive to professional image and appropriate public behavior? Do you cooperate with others? Do you maintain a clean and tidy work space?

▼ Are you approachable? Do you give compliments? Do you communicate with confidence? Maintain an even disposition?

"P" *Provide Information and Rationale*

You should ensure customers' complete understanding. Inform them about what to expect. Use these questions to evaluate yourself in this area:

▼ Are you a good listener? Are you sensitive to customer interests and needs?

▼ Can you deal with differences of opinion? Are you able to compromise?

▼ Do you share information widely?

▼ Are you adequately prepared? Do you anticipate information needs? Do you give ample notice of what's to come, what to expect?

▼ Do you clarify client expectations? (What have they been told?) Do you clarify your expectations and make sure they meet customer needs?

▼ Do you explain procedures and provide a rationale for your business systems?

▼ Do you assist groups with process and task focus?

"R" *Respond to Individualized Needs*

You should be capable of dealing with complex interpersonal relations. While customers may be demanding, they expect a personal response.

▼ Do you approach sensitive situations with people with supportive communication skills? Do you reassure, provide appropriate emotional support, and show empathy?

▼ Do you provide detailed explanations? Do you help identify other resources for solving problems or responding to individual needs?

▼ Do you use active listening skills: paraphrasing, note taking, attending to non-verbal cues?

▼ Do you manage conflict by controlling your own behavior and maintaining a problem solving orientation? Are you tactful with everyone you meet?

▼ Do you have the skills to analyze customer problems? Do you help customers develop options?

▼ Are you sensitive to different cultural or experiential backgrounds?

▼ Do you keep promises made to customers and co-workers?

Summary

Employees are judged first on performance of tasks, and this is as it should be. Thus, to excel in an organization, workers must first earn credibility and trust by getting the job done. Only then can they legitimately expect to exert leadership, influence others, and be considered for promotion. Communication skills play a major role in establishing their credibility. This chapter focused on communication skills and strategies that maximize the probability for organizational success and positive evaluation.

In the following chapters, we build on this foundation to develop a model with the following thesis: individuals can progress as employees through different developmental phases within an organization. Initially, understanding organizational performance expectations allows employees to become functional human resources. Later, as employee task performance stabilizes, greater decision making input, formal and informal group roles, and successful creation and completion of additional opportunities enhance satisfaction and reflect advancement potential. It is important to understand and apply this developmental model to maximize personal empowerment.

Action Contracting

The choice of using communication skills is open to everyone who has learned them. The choice of not using them is also an alternative.

However, people who have chosen not to use their best skills have no one to fault but themselves for not getting or misinterpreting information.

The following "Communication Action Plan" provides opportunity to prepare for a situation in which good communication is vital. It should help you focus on developmental needs for practice or training.

1. Picture a high priority communication situation you anticipate soon.

2. Write down a few key elements that describe the situation. Remember: different perspectives occur in all situations.

3. What will be the best possible outcome? For you? For the other parties (customers, peers)? For the organization?

4. List three possible barriers to the best possible outcome.

5. If you have not listed these above, list two barriers that might come from you (lack of skill, attitude, credibility).

6. Identify three communication skills or strategies you might use to try to overcome or manage the barriers listed above.

7. Which one of the three communication skills or strategies do you anticipate will be most important?

8. Vow to use that skill. Write down this promise to yourself.

9. After the situation, reread your promise and consider honestly how well you fulfilled it.

10. Evaluate the outcome. Was there anything you could have done differently to change the outcome? If so, why didn't you do it? What can you do to assure greater future success with similar situations?

Endnotes Chapter 2

[1]Michael J. Papa and Karen Tracy, "Communicative Indices of Employee Performance with New Technology," *Communication Research,* October, 1988, pp. 524–544; Robert A. Snyder and James H. Morris, "Organizational Communication and Performance," *Journal of Applied Psychology,* Summer, 1984, pp. 461–465.

[2]Teresa M. Harrison, "Communication and Participative Decision Making: An Exploratory Study," *Personnel Psychology,* Winter, 1985, pp. 93–116; Peter R. Monge, S. G. Bachman, J. P. Dillard, and E. M. Eisenberg, "Communicator Competence in the Workplace: Model Testing and Scale Development," in *Communication Yearbook 5,* Michael Burgoon (ed.). New Brunswick, New Jersey: Transaction Books, 1982.

[3]Lawrence R. Wheeless, Virginia Eman Wheeless, and Richard D. Howard, "The Relationships of Communication with Supervisor and Decision-Participation to Employee Job Satisfaction," *Communication Quarterly,* Spring, 1984, pp. 224–231.

[4]"How Does Japan Inc. Pick Its American Workers?" *Business Week,* October 3, 1988, pp. 84–88.

[5]Beverly Davenport Sypher and Theodore E. Zorn, Jr., "Communication-Related Abilities and Upward Mobility: A Longitudinal Investigation," *Human Communication Research,* Spring, 1986, pp. 420–431.

[6]Thomas Owen, "The Self Managing Work Teams," *Small Business Reports,* February, 1991, p. 61.

[7]Jack R. Gibb, "Defensive Communication," *The Journal of Communication,* September, 1961, pp. 141–148.

[8]See for instance, Robert Levering, *A Great Place to Work.* New York: Random House, 1988; Steve Buchholz and Thomas Roth, *Creating The High Performance Team.* New York: John Wiley and Sons, Inc., 1987; Dennis Kinlaw, *Coaching for Commitment.* San Diego: University Associates, 1989; Daniel W. Russell, Elizabeth Altmaier, and Dawn Van Velzen, "Job-Related Stress, Social Support, and Burnout Among Classroom Teachers," *Journal of Applied Psychology,* May, 1987, pp. 269–274; Sandra L. Kirmeyer and Thung-Rung Lin, "Social Support: Its Relationship To Observed Communication With Peers and Superiors," *Academy of Management Journal,* March, 1987, pp. 138–151; Gail Greco, "Teams Score Victories At Work," *Nation's Business,* April, 1988, pp. 38–39.

[9]Gerald M. Goldhaber, Michael P. Yates, D. Thomas Porter, and Richard Lesniak, "Organizational Communication: 1978," *Human Communication Research,* Fall, 1978, p. 83.

[10]Rosabeth Moss Kanter, *The Changemasters.* New York: Simon and Schuster, 1983; Robert Levering, *A Great Place to Work.* New York: Homewood, Illinois: Dow Jones-Irwin, 1987.

[11]The continua as referenced by Gibb are adapted with examples in Les Wallace, "Communicative Approaches to Performance Evaluation," *Supervisory Management*, March, 1978, pp. 2–9.

[12]"New Ways to Exercise Power," *Fortune*, November 6, 1989; "Who Needs a Boss?," *Fortune*, May 7, 1990.

[13]See, for example, J.A. Daly and J.C. McCrosky, Eds., *Avoiding Communication: Shyness, Reticence, and Communication Apprehension.* Beverly Hills, Ca.: Sage, 1984.

[14]Samuel L. Becker and Leah R. V. Ekdom, "That Forgotten Basic Skill: Oral Communication," *Association for Communication Administration Bulletin*, 1980, pp. 12–25.

[15]Papa and Tracy.

[16]See, for example, Charles M. Kelly, "Empathic Listening," in *Small Group Communication: A Reader*, Robert Cathcart and Larry Samovar (eds.). Dubuque, Iowa: Wm. C. Brown Co., 1974, pp. 340–348.

[17]Carl Rogers, *On Becoming a Person.* Boston: Houghton Mifflin, 1961.

[18]Carl R. Rogers and Richard E. Farson, "Active Listening," in *Readings in Interpersonal and Organizational Communication*, Richard C. Huseman, Cal M. Logue, Dwight L. Freshley, (eds.). Boston: Holbrook Press, Inc., 1973.

[19]Gerald M. Goldhaber, *Organizational Communication.* Dubuque, Iowa: Wm. C. Brown Company Publishers, 1983, p. 179.

[20]Dennis D. Phillips, "A Systematic Study of The Leadership Process at the Corporate Level of Two Television Group Owners." Unpublished doctoral dissertation. Athens, OH: Ohio University, 1976.

[21]James W. Fredrickson, "Effects of Decision Motive and Organizational Performance Level on Strategic Decision Processes," *Academy of Management Journal*, December, 1985, pp. 821–843.

[22]For example, see "The Self-Managed Work Team," *Small Business Reports*, February, 1991, pp. 53–65.

[23]David Barry, "Managing the Bossless Team: Lessons in Distributed Leadership," *Organizational Dynamics*, Summer, 1991, p. 34.

[24]For expanded detail based upon primary research, see Norman R. F. Maier, *Problem Solving and Creativity.* Belmont, California: Brooks/Cole Publishing Company, 1970.

[25]J. M. Juran, *Juran on Planning for Quality.* New York: The Free Press, 1988, pp. 26–29.

[26]From "People First: Customer Relations C.P.R."™ Signature Resources 1988.

Chapter

Developing Functional Maturity

"The journey of a thousand miles starts with the first step."
                                                    Chinese Proverb

"I've learned to use the word impossible with the greatest caution."
                                                    Werner von Braun

*". . . anyone over 30 who still wants someone else to give [him/her]
three things to work on over the next twelve months is a pretty
immature adult."*

                                                    Peter Block

Here's a movie we've all seen. Some may have even played a supporting role. New professional, reeking of self confidence and lots of book learned knowledge, enters an organization. New professional is disappointed with the quality, knowledge, and brilliance of others in the organization. Blessed with ideas and suggestions, new professional accelerates from 0–60 in a matter of weeks, making sure everyone knows how "it should be done." Not a good listener, impatient with slow progress, and certain of success, new professional pushes and alienates co-workers and management. How do members of the organization begin referring to new professional behind his/her back? Refer to title. Fast forward to predictable ending.

—"Rebel Without A Clue," Reprinted from *Elan Vital,* Denver: Signature Resources, Fall, 1990.

Newly hired employees have extensive information needs. They also feel the pressure to show they can learn the job and the organizational rules quickly. Regardless of past schooling or experience, most workers find challenges and apprehensions in every new job.

Employee and Professional Development: The *Instructive Phase*

The period of getting up to speed in a new work environment is characterized by particular communication dynamics. We call this the *"Instructive Phase"* of professional development. With much written about "socialization" or "orientation" processes,[1] it is generally understood that positive encounters in the early period of organizational life smooth one's assimilation into the job. Thus, for purposes of self development, it is important to understand early the communication dynamics at work, the expectations of the organization, and how others evaluate employee behavior in determining satisfactory maturation in the job. Even in the first days of organization life, a worker's credibility is being evaluated. In the *instructive phase*, employees must demonstrate task competence as the first step in establishing their personal credibility within the organization.

Expectations in Developing Functional Maturity

Oral and written instructions on what to do and how to do it should supersede all other expectations.

▼ Job Instruction

Employees should receive much information in the *instructive phase*. The primary content should be related to accomplishment: tasks, duties, work habits, interpersonal behaviors, and rules required to produce or serve as expected to by the organization. To create appropriate expectations during this phase, supervisors and trainers tend to be directive (telling vs selling) and rely heavily on written information (manuals and employee handbooks). They frequently focus on five important subjects: job instruction, job rationale, citizenship information (regarding regulations, policies, and benefits), performance feedback, and ideology (information enlisting individual support, loyalty, and morale).[2] They issue commands in two forms: (1) publications and other written material on policies and procedures; and (2) "verbal directives."[3]

▼ Directive Supervision

A few years ago two researchers concluded that managers tend to use coercion with low-trust workers—including new employees.[4] While coercion may be too harsh a word for what happens in most work situations, research indicates that new employees respond best to a supervisory style that is high in structure and task-relevant knowledge.[5] Some supervisors temper this "command information" with more open discussion. When the supervisor encourages questions and comments, the socialization process is improved.[6] People feel better even if the situation is awkward at first. Regardless of the overall supervisory style, however, employees should expect lots of information, structure, and direction early, with most of it related to task accomplishment.

▼ Formal Orientation

In many organizations this "task oriented" and "rule oriented" socialization process involves formal orientation programs. Structured orientation has two distinct tracks: one-on-one task related instruction by supervisors and co-workers, and group briefings on topics such as personnel benefits, general policies, safety, and company history. In smaller organizations, this orientation may be ignored or treated informally. In larger organizations, the formal structure can lead to information overload for the new employee. Union Carbide, for example, once supported its orientation program with a corporate policy notebook of more than 200 pages. Recently the firm reduced this volume of information to a 16-page pamphlet.[7]

▼ Operating Policies

Even with formal orientation programs, not all organizations address specific expectations well. Nevertheless, clearly written position descriptions and skills training are critical. Equally important is a clear delineation of which persons have immediate supervisory responsibility for the job—and who they answer to and who is responsible for their evaluations. There is a true story of a new employee in a retail firm who spent his first month on the job looking for things to do. He became the brunt of private jokes among other workers who watched him take occasional orders from four different supervisors, none of whom told him how to do anything, and none of whom accepted the responsibility for evaluating his performance. The employee wasted his time and that of the company for three months before leaving, at which time he said he never knew what he was supposed to do and never took the time to learn who to ask.[8]

Progressive organizations have a formal phase of orientation at the department level or job site. At this point, employees are provided specific job instruction, the rationale for doing the job right, the personnel policies, and the citizenship expectations within the department. Such specific information allows employees to achieve and excel on a day-to-day basis. Realizing the importance of this, many organizations provide a checklist for auditing expected behavioral outcomes. To assure complete understanding, some organizations require both the supervisor and new employee to sign the checklist. If an organization does not provide such a list, the worker is well advised to develop one through note taking and close attention to detail.

▼ Informal Rules

New employees will also develop relationships with co-workers. The information exchanged through these informal channels will usually be task orientated in nature.[9] Any group activity at this stage will most likely consist of clarifying and elaborating work information. Employees should expect to receive information from the other workers on informal rules and shared values.[10] In less professionally mature work groups, there may be some pressure to limit the quality or productivity of the work of new employees. (We will discuss this pressure in Chapter 6.)

Organizations vary in their commitment to new-worker orientation. Smaller organizations may be limited in their training budgets. No matter! Whether the organization or the employee initiates the information

Assuring Adequate Job Orientation Checklist

✔ Review each major job task to include procedures and outcomes.

✔ Review each duty mentioned in job description.

✔ Review safety policies and procedures.

✔ Review personnel policies.

✔ Review departmental and company organization chart and chain of command.

✔ Identify departmental decision making processes (e.g., handling problems, suggestions, role of work team in decision making).

✔ Review department and organizational objectives.

✔ Review the "Performance Evaluation" form, process and the frequency of employee reviews.

✔ Discuss "supervisor's" expectations for employee behavior and communication.

✔ Review "customer expectation" available regarding your department's product or service.

✔ Review expectations for interdepartmental relationships.

✔ Identify training and developmental opportunities.

exchange, we want to underscore its critical value, and encourage you to expect it.

If employees do not receive good job information, they cannot advance in the organization. Nor can they expect to influence decisions. In fact, to anticipate continued employment would be folly.

Summary of Expectations: *Instructive Phase*

✔ Job instruction specific to tasks, work habits, and quantitative and qualitative performance goals.

✔ Directive supervision with emphasis on providing much information, oral and written, with rationale for techniques, processes, quality and quantity expectations.

✔ Formal orientation that includes organizational ideology, policy, and history.

✔ Operating policies and procedures, work place citizenship expectations.

✔ Informal rules and expectations of co-workers.

Responsibilities: The Roles of Communication

Two responsibilities supersede all others in the instructive phase of employee development:

1. *Understand the job tasks as defined by the organization and the immediate supervisor or team leader.*

2. *Learn to do these tasks competently and in a manner that will please the supervisor.*

▼ Understanding Job Tasks

In the *instructive phase,* employees must learn basic tasks. Listening is paramount, specifically the skills of paraphrasing, asking questions of clarification, note-taking, and summarization. Supervisory rewards and punishments will influence an employee's feeling of confidence and control.[11] Therefore, the employee must clarify and understand expectations in order to enhance the opportunity to achieve, and thus reap the reward. Questioning for clarification can even help the *supervisor* to understand performance standards. It can also diminish bias in formal performance appraisals.[12]

▼ Investing in Analysis of Information

People new on the job can find it difficult to assimilate all the information given them. Because they do not have functional reference points from which to prioritize information, they often choose to ignore much of what gets communicated during orientation. What they fail to consider is that divergence from already established values and protocol will be stressful and usually evaluated negatively. Workers should take time to analyze, clarify, and evaluate information. Doing so sensitizes employees to the organizational reward system and equips them for more informed choices in the use of communication skills and strategies later.

▼ Self Responsibility

What if you do not get a formal orientation? What if you do not get the large quantity of information you anticipate? What if you do not understand the information given? What if, despite careful listening, questioning and paraphrasing, you are not able to get the information you need? Let's consider some alternatives.

1. Do what you think is appropriate and hope you are right.

2. Observe the way others around you are working and what they are accomplishing. Model their behavior.

3. Gather information from any source available. Meanwhile, continue to do what seems appropriate.

4. Find a co-worker who seems to be achieving. Ask for help there.

5. Ask for specifics from the supervisor again. Explain that you need clarification to get the job done right.

6. Do nothing to clarify the task, but complain to fellow workers, your spouse, and friends that the organization does not tell you anything yet they expect you to do the job.

These are not the only alternatives, but they are commonly chosen by workers. The consequences vary. With each alternative, the employee takes risks, and the organizational response is never totally predictable. Possibly, there are no wrong answers. Casual observation in many American organizations suggests that the first alternative is the most often chosen.

There is a better way. Effective workplace communication involves a shared responsibility between managers and those they supervise. And workers need to take the initiative. Early inquiry and clarification assures them of identifying key expectations and getting opportunities to achieve. Further, employees who talk through their difficulties with others will usually be accepted in the organization more readily than those who complain or keep silent.[13] Those who work at clear communication show sincerity in wanting to be part of the team. Merely hoping for the best increases stress and elicits suspicion and negative feedback. Complaining brings on coercion and punishment.

▼ Job Performance

While new workers have many pressures and responsibilities, they will be evaluated on one basic factor in their performance: competence.

Accepting Assignments

Consider the following questions when accepting work assignments or projects:

1. Do you understand the results expected in terms of quality, quantity, and timing?

2. Do you understand the relationship of the assignment to the departmental objectives and goals of the organization?

3. Do you understand how expected outcomes relate to customer expectations? This includes people within the organization and those outside it whose needs are being met by this activity.

4. Are you clear on the resources available to you to complete the work? These include raw materials, supplies, tools and equipment, information, work partners, purchasing authority, and scheduling.

5. Do you have authority to use these resources without checking with someone else? What is the process?

6. What type of feedback is expected from you (problems, delays, new information, milestones) and how often? In what form—oral, written, graphs or financial?

Pleasing supervisors is essential. In most organizations with which we have worked, job performance is the most important determinant of credibility and trust. The ability to do the job well is the key to earning later opportunities.

Many workers have shared with us their frustration with supervisors who are not receptive to new ideas. To an extent, we empathize with people in this situation, but we often see employees trying to effect change before they have earned the right to do so. They need to meet performance expectations consistently over a period of time first. Doing the job better than anyone else remains the best way to create new opportunities.

According to one important study, all peak performers continually evaluate their performance and adjust their efforts and skills to meet expectations.[14] Right from the start, employees should compare their performance regularly with job standards and with their previous performance. Honest introspection helps employees improve on the job.[15] To the extent that they evaluate their past performance as better than average and begin to succeed, they can anticipate celebration and further opportunity.

The organizational literature demands that clear expectations be developed early.[16] If they are not, the result is "powerlessness" and lowering of self-esteem and confidence.[17] Many studies indicate that employees not clear about their roles are more likely to be dissatisfied with their jobs and less capable of meeting good performance expectations.[18] Other studies add that clearly assigned goals and expectations result in less job stress, less boredom, and better satisfaction with performance.[19]

This point is: it is your job and your credibility (competence) being evaluated. So assume 100% of the responsibility to find out what to do and how. Then do it. You should not expect to develop workplace influence nor a sense of satisfaction until you do.

Summary of Responsibilities: *Instructive Phase*

✔ Understand performance expectations, as identified by supervisors.
✔ Analyze information provided.
✔ Evaluate yourself, seek feedback, listen carefully and ask questions.
✔ Fulfill basic performance expectations in task, work habit, and interpersonal arenas.

Celebration

Acknowledgement for doing the job as expected should serve as the basic form of celebration in achieving competence in task-related performance.

During the 1980's, Tom Peters and Nancy Austin wrote extensively about business conditions and the needs of the American worker to enjoy and be challenged by work:

> All of us learn how to enjoy things before the age of six. And then we observe joy later on—among the members of the country's top Girl Scout cookie-selling troop and the city's top youth league soccer team, at the top Limited store, the top Wang sales branch and in the bakery crew at Stew Leonard's 'Disneyland of Dairy Stores.' But all too often our instinct for zest is driven out of us by our formal education, especially professional education. Life, and surely life in organizations, is not supposed to be fun.
>   . . . And yet time and again, whether the evidence is the unit flags on the flight line at the Tactical Air Command or the smiles on the

faces of the people at Nordstrom's [Department Store], we've observed that winners are people who have fun— and produce results as a result of their zest.[20]

We hear employees ask: "How can I enjoy work and have fun when the organization doesn't recognize my contributions?" Or say, "I make one mistake and my supervisor is all over my back, but I never hear anything about all the good things that I do."

▼ Acknowledgement

What is celebration? Why do we need it? Will it mean that we will have to do more in the future? How will co-workers react? At this phase of organizational development, we believe celebration means being recognized for a job well done. Such acknowledgment improves performance and increases motivation.[21] Employees should expect the celebration, though, only after a job has actually been done well. Displays of appreciation and consideration before warranted by performance send improper signals.[22] And long hours and hard work are not reasons to celebrate; they are not reasons for positive job evaluation. Performance (expected outcomes achieved), as expected by the supervisor and the organization, is the reason for celebration. Indeed, in more sophisticated organizations, work teams will have plenty of feedback on the quality and quantity of work and may see such results posted.

▼ Diplomatic Self Publicity

What if celebration is deserved and not forthcoming? Few employees feel their boss provides enough appreciation for the job they do.[23] However, each employee needs to honestly answer some key questions: Was the achievement a performance expectation? Was it actually that good? Did you contribute significant value toward accomplishment? Did anyone know of the accomplishment? Did the right people know?

Pats on the back, the supervisor's voiced appreciation for a job well done, positive strokes from co-workers—these are elements of celebration in the early stages of organizational development. For most people, they feel good. Many people fret when they do not get such rewards but they tend to sit idly by rather than doing anything about it. When compliments are not forthcoming, and workers honestly believe they are deserved, they need to publicize themselves to the people that count—proactive communication. A diplomatic strategy for gaining recognition is to ask for feedback from your supervisor: "How am I doing?" "Am I doing the job right?" "What am I not doing well?" "What am I not doing that I should be doing?"

When a task is completed and done well, asking for supervisory comments at that point may reduce stress over lack of recognition. "Did you know that I . . . ? Is that OK?" Some argue that this is begging for compliments or inappropriate in their positions. This is not true. Research indicates that seeking feedback helps determine needed corrections to performance and provides information for reaching valued ends,[24] and more frequent feedback tends to be related to better performance.[25] Be forewarned, though. A supervisor may not perceive the accomplishments positively. Or, it may not have been a job-related priority. However, the advantage in speaking up like this is gaining understanding that otherwise might not be received until it is too late.

Lack of feedback may mean the supervisor actually has not noticed. Or more likely, the supervisor noticed but did not see a need to respond.[26] Employees can wait for the yearly appraisal. But why? We think it makes much more sense to seek out the supervisor and obtain the information for celebration right away, rather than withdrawing and feeling sorry for the perceived lack of appreciation.

Summary of Celebration: *Instructive Phase*

✔ Supervisory acknowledgement, anticipate positive feedback.
✔ Diplomatic self publicity, clarification of satisfactory performance: "How do you think I'm doing?"

Instructive Phase: New and Seasoned Employees

New employees are always in the *instructive phase* of development until their competence in both task and organizational citizenship are demonstrated. Typically, the average to above average employee will move beyond this stage sometime within the first one to six months of employment in a new organization—three months on the average. However, new employees are not the only workers who project behaviors that warrant instruction or compliance oriented supervisory communication. Experienced workers who do not understand the changing expectations of the organization, workers who do not have the skills or training to keep pace with the organizational expectations, workers whose priorities lie exclusively outside the organization, and workers whose goals are disruptive to the organization might also need correction. Table 1 at the end of this chapter identifies behaviors characteristic of employees (new employees and veterans) whose work behavior elicits and warrants more directive supervision. Employees displaying these behaviors will be subjected to closer supervision and have few opportunities.

Why might employees who are not new to the organization display less mature performance behavior? There are many reasons. Job expectations have changed, and such workers are unable to keep up or were not informed (nor did they ask). They have become frustrated or burned out with the job. Problems away from the job are depleting their energy. They have not been rewarded either with pay or positive reinforcement (and they probably have not actively sought it). They do not know why someone else was promoted to or reassigned to the position they wanted, or they do not accept the decision (and perhaps they have not asked for an explanation of it). They feel stifled by the organization and the supervisor, so they are angry. Also, they may not have assessed possible new opportunities in the situation. Or they may simply be rebellious.

Such attitudes and behaviors occur in all organizations in both novice and experienced employees. Each of us has control over our own behavior, however. In the organization, those doing the job right are generally the ones rewarded, if not with money, with positive reinforcement, credibility, trust, and freedom to operate independently—in other words, personal empowerment.

Summary of *Instructive Phase*

It is not unusual for employees to feel ''powerlessness'' in the early stages of organizational development. Low task variety, inflexible routines, strict supervisors, rule structure, and a clearly defined regiment should be expected.[27] Remember, task accomplishment should be the single overriding concern of employees in these early stages of employment.

Beyond initial performance, however, initiating additional inquiry, paying attention to new information sources and leaders can yield information to identify additional workplace opportunities. By being an astute listener, one can uncover unwritten rules and informal power structures. Observing communication procedures in formal and informal groups can reveal how decisions are made. Seeking out more information on organizational goals is an intelligent tactic. During this early phase of development, employees should regularly review the orientation checksheet to assure that they understand and are still meeting the expectations. Initiating supervisory feedback, prioritizing the tasks as the boss sees them, taking notes, comparing understandings, asking if there is anything else to be done—all maximize the potential for success. Performance is the key to greater work freedom and influence; information is the key to opportunity. At the end of this chapter you will find some suggested targets for building skills and organizational perspective (Table 2).

Work can be as much fun and as fulfilling as play.[28] What we forget is that we need to make it fun. We do that by being proactive communicators, listening, and asking for opportunities that we want; then doing the job . . . better than anyone else . . . after we have proven that we can do the job expected.

Some people go to work and get paid so they can have fun.

Others have fun and get paid for it as work.

Which do you prefer? A worker who fulfills the responsibilities of the *instructive phase* of development, appropriately initiates celebration and assesses opportunities is working toward the second scenario.

Consider some examples of phase one employees:

Darryl: Case History of Employee Failure

Darryl was an admissions clerk for a 150-bed metropolitan general hospital. During his employment interview he displayed an outgoing personality, and he showed a particular flair for welcoming guests into the hospital. While working at the hospital, he received many letters and notes of appreciation from patients who appreciated his congeniality and positive outlook.

On the surface, it seemed Darryl was a model employee. Why, then was he asked to leave within a year? His supervisor offered the following: "Darryl never performed the total range of tasks for which he was hired. He jumped at every opportunity to provide a wheelchair escort for guests and spent extraordinary amounts of time assisting others in the hospital with miscellaneous problems and tasks, to the sacrifice of required paperwork and admissions procedures. He regularly had 'better ideas,' mostly in the form of complaints, for the department. I finally had to dismiss him for not doing his job. For me, it was a very unenviable situation of dealing with an extremely popular employee who was performing admirably in virtually every respect except what he was hired to do."

Did Darryl have appropriate and sufficient explanation of job requirements and supervisory expectations? According to the supervisor: "He should have. The job was not difficult. No, I didn't tell him what I needed him to do daily—he was always so busy working with someone else. But, I did remind him during orientation and at his 90-day review. Then, when he still didn't get any better, I monitored his deficiencies regularly. His six month performance review was not pretty. I had to be directive and very specific."

Darryl offered the following informally to other employees while he was still working: "I really like working here. Everyone is so nice and helpful—except my supervisor. She rarely speaks to me, and when she does, it's bawling me out."

Did Darryl seek out clarification and specifics regarding performance expectations from the one person responsible for his continued employ? No. Did he heed the performance feedback and concentrate on his primary task accomplishment to show the boss he could do the work? No.

Brenda: Case History of Empowered Employee Achievement

Brenda has been with a computer development firm nearly five years. Her first supervisor recalls: "Brenda came to the company with great credentials, but she was very quiet, almost to the point of being standoffish. The only time she spoke was to ask questions: 'What is my role on this production team?' 'Why do we use our current procedure to mount chips on PC boards?' I loved her attitude, though. She really meant business. When I showed her how we do things, she'd thank me, ask if I would watch her work for a little bit, and tell her how she was doing. I found out that she didn't need much help. In fact, she showed me within the first six months that she was a great technician, and I tried to let her know that I appreciated it. Of course, I lost her before long."

Brenda not only was a fine technician, but also a problem solver whose ideas have been innovative and yet inexpensive to the firm. Her supervisor lost her because she was promoted. She has since been promoted a second time in less than five years with the organization.

Did her supervisor provide on site instruction and training? Did Brenda get appropriate and sufficient information to do the job? Did Brenda clarify and actively seek out expectations? Did her attention to "knowing the job first" lead to new opportunities? Did she earn the credibility to be allowed to influence the organization? The answer to all of the above is yes.

TABLE 1
Employee Behaviors Characteristic of the *Instructive Phase**

▼ Lacks complete job knowledge.

▼ Brags about effort rather than accomplishment.

▼ May slow down in the absence of a supervisor.

▼ Inconsistent productivity.

▼ Frequently waits to be told what to do next.

▼ Reluctant to accept additional tasks.

▼ Has difficulty meeting deadlines; needs help organizing regular work.

▼ Does not assist others without being asked.

▼ May have problems with work habits (attendance, tardiness, personal appearance, gossiping).

▼ Takes shortcuts by bending the policies and procedures.

▼ Always asks before taking action; reluctant to take independent responsibility for decisions.

▼ Reluctant to cooperate with other team members.

▼ Depends upon supervisor for information obtainable elsewhere through independent inquiry.

▼ Shows little interest in the rationale behind the way things are done.

▼ Criticizes without offering suggestions.

▼ Uncertain of the decision-making process.

▼ Unable to evaluate his/her own performance objectively.

▼ Uncertain about long term professional goals.

▼ Tense and uncomfortable with adversity and stress.

▼ Reluctant to change; resists/pouts about change.

▼ Displays poor customer relations skills.

☐ **Development Check:** Have you taken action to assure the information, skills/competencies and self responsibilities necessary to earn greater opportunity for influence?

*Supervisors across the country tell us that these behaviors are signs that workers may still be in an *instructive phase* of development.

TABLE 2
Building Skills and Organizational Perspective

Improvement Targets for *Instructive Phase*
1. Listening skills.
2. Clarifying task information and assignments.
3. Problem analysis and definition.
4. Communication sending skills.
5. Work place rules and procedures.
6. Organizational structure and chain of command.
7. Task procedures and requirements.
8. Assertiveness.
9. Customer relations skills.

Suggested Readings
▼ All handbooks, publications and product/service materials of your company.

▼ Christopher Hegarty, *How To Manage Your Boss*. Mill Valley, CA: Whatever Publishing, 1982.

▼ Pamela Schockley-Zalabak, *Fundamentals of Organizational Communication*. NY: Longman, 1988.

▼ Kathleen Verderber and Rudolph Verderber, *Interact: Using Interpersonal Skills*. Belmont, CA: Wadsworth, 1989.

Endnotes Chapter 3

[1]Fredric M. Jablin, "Task/Work Relationships: A Life-Span Perspective," *Foundations of Organizational Communication*, Steven R. Corman, Stephen P. Banks, Charles R. Bantz, and Micheal E. Mayer (eds.). New York: Longman, 1990, pp. 171–196; Fredric M. Jablin, "Superior-Subordinate Communication: The State of the Art," *Psychological Bulletin*, November, 1979, pp. 1201–1222; James R. Terborg, "Women in Management: A Research Review," *Journal of Applied Psychology*. December, 1977, pp. 647–664; Daniel Charles Feldman, "The Multiple Socialization of Organizational Members," *Academy of Management Review*, April, 1967, pp. 309–318.

[2]Daniel Katz and Robert Kahn, *The Social Psychology of Organizations*. New York: John Wiley, 1978.

[3]Charles Conrad, *Strategic Organizational Communication: Cultures, Situations, and Adaptation*. New York: Holt, Rinehart and Winston, 1985, pp. 8–9.

[4]Samuel C. Riccillo and Sarah Trendholm, "Predicting Managers' Choice of Influence Mode: The Effects of Interpersonal Trust and Worker Attributes on Managerial Tactics in a Simulated Organizational Setting," *Western Journal of Speech Communication*, Fall, 1983, pp. 323–339.

[5]Robert P. Vecchio, "Situational Leadership Theory: An Examination of a Prescriptive Theory," *Journal of Applied Psychology*, August, 1987, pp. 444–451.

[6]F. Dansereau, J. Cashman, and G. Graen, "Instrumentality Theory and Equity Theory as Complementary Approaches in Predicting the Relationship of Leadership and Turnover among Managers," *Organizational Behavior and Human Performance*, 1975, pp. 46–78.

[7]Jayne Landon, "International Business Communication," unpublished Master's thesis, Colorado State University, Spring, 1988, p. 24.

[8]For those who consider this an isolated incident, see: John Hoerr, "With Job Training, A Little Dab Won't Do Ya," *Business Week*, September 24, 1990; Benjamin Benson, "Do You Keep Too Many Secrets?" *Nation's Business*, August, 1989, pp. 42–44.

[9]D. C. Feldman and J. M. Brett, "Coping with New Jobs: A Comparative Study of New Job Hires and Job Changers," *Academy of Management Journal*, 1983, pp. 258–272.

[10]D. C. Feldman, "The Development and Enforcement of Group Norms," *Academy of Management Review, 1984, pp. 47–53.*

[11]David B. Greenberger, Stephen Strasser, Soonmook Lee, "Personal Control as a Mediator Between Perceptions of Supervisory Behaviors and Employee Reactions," *Academy of Management Journal*, June, 1988, pp. 405–417.

[12]Joseph M. Czajka and Angelo S. DeNisi, "Effects of Emotional Disability and Clear Performance Standards on Performance Ratings," *Academy of Management Journal*, June, 1988, pp. 394–404.

[13]Fredric M. Jablin, "Organizational Entry, Assimilation, and Exit," *Handbook of Organizational Communication*, Fredric M. Jablin, Linda L. Putnam, Karlene H. Roberts, and Lyman W. Porter (eds.). Newbury Park, California: Sage Publications, Inc., 1987, pp. 679–740.

[14]Charles Garfield, *Peak Performers*. New York: Avon Books, 1986.

[15]Donald J. Campbell and Cynthia Lee, "Self-Appraisal in Performance Evaluation: Development Versus Evaluation," *Academy of Management Review*, April, 1988, pp. 302–314.

[16]Chris D. Orth, Harry E. Wilkinson, and Robert C. Benfori, "The Manager's Role as Coach and Mentor," *Organizational Dynamics*, March, 1987, pp. 66–74; Marion E. Haynes, "Partnership in Management: Employee Involvement Gets Results," *Personnel Journal*. July, 1986, pp. 46–55; George Doran, "Manager As Coach;" *Working Women*, January, 1984, pp. 16–19.

[17]Jay A. Conger and Rabindra N. Kanungo, "The Empowerment Process: Integrating Theory and Practice," *Academy of Management Review*, July, 1988, pp. 471–482.

[18]Ajay K. Kohli, "Some Unexplored Supervisory Behaviors and Their Influence on Salespeople's Role Clarity, Specific Self-Esteem, Job Satisfaction, and Motivation," *Journal of Marketing Research*, November, 1985, pp. 424–433.

[19]Sam E. White, Terence R. Mitchell, and Cecil H. Bell, Jr., "Goal Setting, Evaluation Apprehension, and Social Cues as Determinants of Job Performance and Job Satisfaction in a Simulated Organization," *Journal of Applied Psychology*, December, 1977, pp. 665–673; Gary Hunt and Ruby Ebeling, "The Impact of an Employee Communication Program on Work Group Productivity," paper presented to Western Speech Communication Association, Albuquerque, New Mexico, February, 1983.

[20]Tom Peters and Nancy Austin, *A Passion for Excellence*. New York: Warner Books, Inc., 1985, p. 296.

[21]Thomas E. Becker and Richard J. Klimoski, "A Field Study of the Relationship Between the Organizational Feedback Environment and Performance," *Personnel Psychology*, Summer, 1989, pp. 343–358; Beth Brophy, "The Rite of Annual Reviews," *U.S. News and World Report*, February 3, 1986, p. 59;

[22]Vecchio, p. 449.

[23]Christopher Hegarty, *How To Manage Your Boss*. Mill Valley, California: Whatever Publishing, Inc., 1982, p. 127.

[24]S. J. Ashford, "Feedback Seeking in Individual Adaptation: A Resource Perspective," *Academy of Management Journal*, 1986, pp. 465–487.

[25]Doris M. Cook, ''The Impact on Managers of Frequency of Feedback,'' *Academy of Management Journal*, 1968, pp. 263–278.

[26]Kenneth A. Kovach, ''What Motivates Employees? Workers and Supervisors Give Different Answers,'' *Business Horizons.* 1988, pp. 58–65; ''Motivation and Morale,'' *Dale Carnegie Institute, Management Class Manual*, 1988, pp. 2–3.

[27]Conger and Kanungo.

[28]Douglas McGregor, *The Human Side of Enterprise.* New York: McGraw-Hill Book Company, 1961, p. 47.

Chapter

Beyond Functional Job Maturity: Interactive Requirements and Opportunities

"We must overcome the notion that we must be regular . . . it robs you of the chance to be extraordinary and leads to the mediocre."

Uta Hagen

"The people who get on in this world are the people who get up and look for circumstances they want, and, if they can't find them, make them"

George Bernard Shaw

"If you don't place your foot on the rope, you'll never cross the chasm."

Liz Smith

There's an old story about a young man who spent a week's paycheck to buy his mother a bird that could speak 10 languages. The day after he had it delivered to her as a gift, he called hoping his mother would enrapture him with gratitude.

"Mom, how did you like the bird?"

"It was delicious."

"You ate it?!? Mom! That bird cost me a week's pay. It spoke 10 languages."

"Well, if it was so smart, why didn't it say something?"

We know a lot of those birds. How many times have you thought of a good idea? Or needed to share a concern? On the job? Interdepartmentally? Field to office? Person to person? But didn't say anything?

Somebody has to say something. Management techniques may help us: open door policies, wandering management, suggestion boxes, quality circles, opinion surveys. But somebody still has to take the initiative. Somebody has to speak up! Just do it!

—"Just Do It!" Reprinted from *Elan Vital*. Denver: Signature Resources, Fall, 1989.

Earning Opportunity

All work and no play make Jack and Jill dull people. And career progress is based on a similar premise. While meeting job expectations is an on-going requirement, good performance ought to earn employees the credibility and trust to speak up and be heard. Many bosses, however, still don't want the individual worker to think but rather to act like a good "team player in the sheep factory . . . following the manager blissfully and ignorantly down the path to dependency and mediocrity."[1] Whether this is your boss, or you are fortunate in working in a more enlightened corporate culture, our research indicates that your influence can be felt in the workplace if you learn to use good interpersonal skills and continue to stretch yourself.

Continual self evaluation enables workers to monitor their performance and the degree to which management recognizes it. Fulfilling expectations brings additional information, responsibility, and opportunity. Because the time frame for the evolution of credibility varies within departments and across organizations, employees need to be sensitive and patient. Nevertheless, as performance improves and experience and training are gained, the organizational role earned by the individual changes though sometimes the employee needs to push. New responsibilities usually require more sophisticated interpersonal and communication behavior.

This chapter focuses on expectations, responsibilities, and opportunities for employees after they have proved that they can fulfill—even exceed—basic job requirements. As they earn functional maturity on the job, they enter a new phase of employee progression: the *interactive phase*.

Expectations in Developing *Interactive* Maturity

Participation in formal and informal group processes becomes a primary expectation for employees who have proven their basic competence. The more trustworthy and personable they are, the more their peers and supervisors will see that they deserve greater responsibilities.

▼ Performance Evaluation: Motivators

As job performance improves, an employee should expect less specific instruction and different responses from supervisors. Feedback frequently becomes less evaluative, more supportive, and may be combined with broader departmental evaluation information through a combination of channels.[2] Positive reinforcement and greater participation in departmental affairs are typical rewards at this stage.[3]

Some positive (and negative) job feedback then should be expected as a staple of everyday (or at least weekly) communication with supervision. While we would like to say that employees should expect to receive positive feedback from employers every time it is earned, and while we would like to say that positive reinforcement will serve as motivators for everyone, the reality of organizational life is different.

In the first place, supervisors in most organizations, even those that value employees, simply do not do a good job of praising people for excellent work. They forget; they get too busy; they displace praise when they speak of employees in glowing terms to other supervisors, top management, and even people outside the organization and not to the employees themselves; they think employees should know; they do not think it's important; or, in some cases, they believe the only good feedback an employee needs is the paycheck.[4] In contrast, unsolicited comments from supervisors occur more often after deviations from standard expectations—that is, mistakes. In those situations, unquestionably, employees can expect to hear "an earful." By implication, however, as employees learn the job, they ought to expect to be their own best evaluators of basic performance. To the extent that they fulfill this expectation honestly and satisfy their own best judgment, they can minimize the negative comments from supervision.

Also, pats on the back do not always motivate. Employees (children, students, middle and top management, people in all walks of life) generally do not recognize positive comments as readily as they do the negative. Kenneth Blanchard suggests that workers require four positive strokes for each one negative comment in order to even realize that they have been praised at all.[5]

▼ Broader Organizational Perspectives

Regarding other expectations, employees should expect to receive more information about the organization and their specific department. This extends beyond just productivity information. It includes what organizational theorists have referred to as ideology: information enlisting individual support, loyalty, and morale.[6] For instance, employees should expect to learn how the company is contributing to the community, what customers are saying about products and services, sales and growth accomplishment, significant positive changes in the organization, and general long range plans.

▼ Participation in Formal Decision Making Processes

Employees may also see opportunities to make suggestions for making the job easier, solving problems, and generating new ideas. More progressive organizations will encourage employee involvement.[7] In most cases, however, employees may expect that supervisors will retain the responsibility for making final decisions. In others, quality improvement teams will have greater decision making autonomy.

When employees do contribute ideas, they can expect a variety of responses. As in the case of positive feedback on job performance, supervisors generally do a poor job following up on employee ideas. Many times supervisors do not recognize the importance of interim feedback or updates. In other cases supervisors are uncomfortable telling employees that their ideas were not considered or were considered but rejected. So what happens is a sort of "pocket veto"[8]—the supervisor says nothing, letting the employee wonder for an infinite amount of time until finally the interest is gone.

▼ Group Involvement

In addition to formal communication channels, employees can also expect to become involved in the informal groups within departments or elsewhere in the organization. Excessive aggressiveness and unwillingness to listen are not likely to lead to group acceptance. However, supportiveness and friendly communication help one gain entry. Later, we elaborate on other ways to ensure such involvement. Group leadership roles at this phase of development center around facilitation of information exchange, gatekeeping, and encouraging the involvement of other workers. At this point, suffice it to say that employees sensitive to their group capabilities should expect additional opportunity to take the lead.

An organization with a strong commitment to innovation and developing personnel will likely be quick to solicit the ideas of employees once they have proved themselves on the job. On the other hand, an organization with a dominant top level and an autocratic history will probably not welcome employee involvement. Employee expectations need not change. However, the responsibilities and the strategies to be used to contribute beyond the basic job performance will.[9]

Summary of Expectations: *Interactive Phase*

✔ Performance evaluation.
✔ Material to broaden organizational perspective, ideology information.
✔ Participation in formal processes, including input into decisions.
✔ Involvement in informal activity and group functioning, opportunity for shared group leadership.

Responsibilities: The Roles of Communication

As employees demonstrate work-related competence, organizational responsibilities expand. Employees should begin to feel "empowered" to speak up and identify problems. They should propose solutions for every problem identified, offering rationale in each case. Employees who argue that it is management's job to solve problems have not accepted the responsibilities of this phase of their development.

▼ Basic Competence

At the *interactive phase* of employee development (as at all phases of organizational life), we believe that basic tasks remain an essential responsibility. Thus, even as employees do more, they reflect credibility first and foremost by performing the job requirements as expected by supervisory staff. Table 3 at the end of this chapter presents a list of behaviors that characterize employees in the *interactive phase*. The list emphasizes people's efforts to initiate communication both for purposes of task accomplishment and team building. However, even as expectations for interpersonal competence increase, task performance remains prominent in the behaviors identified.

▼ Seeking Rationale

Listening skills remain important in the *interactive phase*. Listening for feedback on job performance requires particular sensitivity. When information is not offered, it is important to seek clarification, summarize interpretations, and ask questions. At this stage one question becomes particularly important: "why?" An employee having performed the basic requirements of the job earns the right to hear decisions, policies and procedures explained. Greater understanding of "rationale" enables employees to see the bigger picture, the "organizational perspective." Understanding the broader backdrop increases one's potential to make a valued contribution.

▼ Participation: Dealing in Solutions

Phillips and Wallace[10] present a series of questions for employees to consider when they make suggestions. The questions are based upon the premise that the best ideas help the organization achieve its objectives or improve the work atmosphere. Selling ideas requires planning. One must consider their feasibility and implementation in the workplace. Bringing in ideas also involves the skills of persuasion. When a person makes a good suggestion, it will produce at least some talk with management and usually more and more discussion with peers. As more progressive businesses move toward employee involvement programs, each employee will find greater opportunities for peer influence.[11]

Offering solutions, agenda items, and suggestions that result in benefits may mean additional work. The work comes in the form of researching ideas and working out solutions as identified earlier, as well as in the form of special task force, quality team and committee membership and followup to others. Some people argue that the additional work is not part of their job descriptions and are reluctant to participate. And indeed, some people do get "committeed" to death. However, extra involvement can add a sense of excitement, diversity, enrichment, satisfaction, control, and even motivation to the work experience. It contributes to a feeling of commitment. It adds a dimension of challenge, and of "play," which keeps work from becoming dull. It also generates supervisory trust. And supervisors who trust their workers will enlist their participation. In contrast to autocracy and coercion, the participative styles encourage additional contributions as well as future freedoms and celebration.

Participation: Impact of Organizational Culture

Let's consider employee involvement within two organizational cultures: one participative, the other autocratic.

In the participative culture, employees are sought out for input. They are held accountable for sharing and analyzing information and perspective. Therefore, they need to learn problem-solving and decision analysis skills. In a more mature participative environment, supervisors demonstrate patience and work to "teach" employees how to interact and be involved. Employees are "invited" to share ideas, and the supervisor or team facilitator coaches them in doing so. In very progressive organizations, self directed work teams are trained in the problem solving, influence and team process skills needed to manage their own work.[12] As the employee and work teams improve in making suggestions, they see better responses to their ideas. Obviously, an employee can "fast-track" the contributory process by developing clear rationale for ideas and including details for their implementation. When sound ideas come forth, both the individual and the organization benefit.[13]

The ideal state, however, is seldom actualized.[14] The employee often needs to initiate the process, offering ideas ("What about this?"), listening for comment, fine-tuning the suggestion, listening for comment, testing rationale, and generally "learning the ropes" of contribution. The more participative the organization, the less threatening it is. The key for the employee in this phase of organizational development is to continue developing skills and capabilities to lead the work group creatively.

In a more autocratic culture (and with some supervisors in participative organizations), management may not actively solicit new ideas nor be receptive to suggestions. They may even try to stifle expression. Under these circumstances, strategy must change: employees must create opportunities. To do so, more preparation for the presentation of ideas is necessary. It is important to do homework on organizational values and supervisory preferences before discussing ideas. This means paying attention to all employee manuals and organizational histories, gathering factual data regarding problems, and identifying opinion leaders for support.[15] While preparation is important, a supportive, team attitude is crucial. In an organization less open to employee ideas, anything less than supportive communication is likely to be perceived as hostile and will result in tighter closure of the channels of communication and greater resistance to change. In gathering and preparing information and suggestions, special care must be given to presenting objective data and identifying potential benefits. Take ideas one at a time, focusing on the most critical work priorities or on those with the greatest likelihood for management response. As the first one or two attempts prove successful or the supervisor sees your desire to help the organization, your personal credibility will increase.

All kinds of organizations can suffer from insufficient supervisory feedback and followup. But if employees sit back and let their ideas die, they may grow stagnant or frustrated in their ability to contribute. Thus, employees must create their own followup, seeking diplomatically to learn not only what the decision was, but how and why it was made. Better understanding of the decision making process will improve one's ability to "sell" ideas the next time around.

All this is to say that one can learn to "manage" or "teach" the boss. With appropriate preparation and support, knowledge of the organization and its reward structure, and understanding of supervisory motives, employees can effectively serve as behavioral models for their supervisors. (Chapter 6 has a more complete exploration of selling ideas.)

Some workers will believe that the effort to do this, especially in the autocratic organization, is too great. Unquestionably personal goals and motives need examination here as workers have available some of the same communication choices identified in the preceding chapter. Those who choose to make work as fun and challenging as possible will choose similar communication behaviors and will probably progress in the organization.

▼ Teamwork Expectations

Before we leave the discussion of strategies and skills, let's discuss communication with peers. The organizational research literature identifies work unit communication as a major point of satisfaction for workers across all types of organizations.[13] In recent years organizational managers have seen group communication and teamwork as a key to product and service quality. The reference is usually made in such situations to "total quality management," or "continuous quality improvement," where teams are formed in an overall atmosphere of employee involvement ("EI"). Employees at this phase of development must be adept at group skills and accept responsibility for teamwork.

What exactly is teamwork? How does one behave as an effective team member? In most organizations this is not clearly defined.

Managing Your Supervisor/Team Leader: Guidelines Checklist

1. My supervisor and I meet at least twice a year to discuss long term departmental plans and my specific performance objectives.

2. My supervisor/team leader is aware of all of my ideas for changing and improving our organization/department even if some can't be implemented now.

3. When I take problems to my supervisor, team or others, I'm diplomatic and always prepared to recommend solutions.

4. I have made my supervisor/team leader aware of the type of information about the business that I need in order to do my job better.

5. I am aware of areas where my performance could be improved and have identified a plan of action to improve.

6. I alert my supervisor/team leader to work problems or pressures before they become major.

7. I update my supervisor/team leader on major projects or tasks without being asked.

8. I contribute to our business "team" effort by displaying open and cooperative communication with all persons connected to our business.

9. I am consistently mindful of appropriate customer relations when dealing with persons who do business with us (internal and external customers).

10. My supervisor/team leader and I frequently identify projects or tasks that I am able to accomplish independently or with minimal supervision.

Supervisors and work teams cannot be effective unless they agree on what is meant by teamwork. In progressive environments, work teams may even develop a "code of conduct" to guide cooperative behavior. Consider the following among the key communication behaviors and skills reflective of teamwork:

a. Openly share information others need to enhance their contributions (*supportive communication style and language; open information sharing; concise sending skills; internal customer needs*).

b. Work with ideas of others to find effective and efficient answers (*effective listening; conflict management skills; problem solving skills*).

c. Openly receive, clarify and respect the comments and reactions of others (*supportive communication style; withhold evaluation; group leadership communication skills; conflict management; culture and experienced based sensitivity*).

d. Frequently check commonality of focus between self and others (*clarifying skills; initiating communication skills; internal customer needs*).

e. Ask for assistance, clarification or information when it is needed (*initiating communication skills; disagreeing with diplomacy* [see chapter 6]).

f. Provide positive reinforcement to team members as appropriate (*supportive communication style; conflict management; feedback skills*).

g. Focus comments on ideas, not persons (*supportive communication style; disagreeing with diplomacy* [see chapter 6]).

h. Deal in solutions; fix don't blame (*selling ideas and suggestions; supportive communication* [see chapter 6]).

As employees attempt to develop and solidify their team status, they must behave consistent with the expectations of both management and peer team members. Remember, your co-workers are looking for the elements of personableness and trustworthiness in you.

▼ Interdepartmental Contacts

In the *interactive phase* an employee should get to know people other than the immediate work group. Networking in other departments reveals intricacies of the organization, including (in large organizations) how the work efforts of different units add to the whole of organizational

Team Behavior Checklist

Use the behavioral list started below to provide your teams with greater detail in teamwork expectations. Add other task related behaviors relevant to your work place.

1. Meets team timelines and expectations for task accomplishment and information sharing.

2. Openly shares information others need to enhance their contributions.

3. Deals in solutions and generates multiple options rather than focusing on problems and criticism.

4. Works with the ideas of others to find good solutions to problems.

5. Takes initiative in working out conflicts with team members.

6. Works congenially despite personal feelings about other team members.

7. Frequently checks team agreement and commonality of focus.

8. Openly receives, clarifies and respects the comments and reactions of others.

9. Focuses on objectives through pertinent comments and ideas.

10. Maintains emotional equilibrium in the face of varied behaviors/reactions of team members.

11. Supports other team members during difficult task or emotional periods.

12. Encourages open discussion.

13. Praises other team members as appropriate.

14. Seeks opinions from team members.

15. Readily asks for assistance, clarification or information when in need.

16. Levels with other team members about decisions, performance and contributions.

17. Treats other team members consistently and fairly; respects their feelings and emotions.

18. Confronts inappropriate team behavior in a timely and objective manner.

19. Willing to stick with difficult positions and ideas objectively to ensure breadth of thought.

20. Models appropriate interpersonal relations when dealing with others outside the team.

21. Supports team decisions and contributes to successful implementation.

22. Willing to take on a variety of responsibilities within the team.

achievement. It can also open up lengthier career paths, lateral and upward moves, and educational opportunities.[17]

Internal networking has more subtle benefits as well. As consultants, we frequently hear employees claim their organization has poor interdepartmental communication. We have found no magic formula for enhancing these deficiencies except that someone must initiate cross-departmental communication. Remember other departments may serve as customers or vendors. Talking with vendors assists them with better service. Talking with customers assures clarification of expected quality. The networking process not only adds to the mental library of information for present and future personal development, but also enhances interdepartmental relations.

Summary of Responsibilities: *Interactive Phase*

✔ Continued performance competence.
✔ Seeking rationale for performance, technique, and process.
✔ Participation, initiating ideas, dealing in solutions, problem solving skills and tools.
✔ Teamwork, shared team leadership.
✔ Interdepartmental contacts for investigating and clarifying internal customer needs, greater organizational performance perspective, career planning, broader personal influence.

Celebration

Depending upon the policies of an organization, rewards in the interactive phase might include bonuses and raises. However, there may also be nonmonetary rewards such as opportunities to offer decision making input, seeing ideas and information utilized, more challenging and satisfying work, continued positive feedback on job performance, and integration into the social functioning of group membership.

▼ Material Reward

Bonuses or pay increases are material representations of celebration. Students, particularly remind us of money as an essential element of anticipated reward. The productivity survey of the Industrial Engineers has recently identified money as a critical motivator.[18] If nothing else, money serves to enhance status and security. Therefore, it is central in the reward structure in most American organizations.

While money is important, most research presents monetary rewards in a different light.[19] Money, as a means of celebration, is impersonal and short lived. Money seldom brings full satisfaction. Further, it often establishes jealousies and competition because it seems there is never enough for everyone. There is no consistent body of literature that shows money, once received, creates any future motivation. Finally, many organizations are so tight with their money that it is unrealistic to hope for any meaningful contribution of money other than as a token. So we see other rewards as equal to, and possibly greater than, money.

▼ Training and Development

Organizations frequently reward good work and leadership behavior through opportunity for further training or development. Employees should take advantage of every developmental opportunity offered by the company. Such training is part of the trend toward lifelong learning, and in the next decade it will become a necessity for employability. Indeed, part of celebration may involve employees expressing interest in further training or education and asking how the company might help.

▼ Employee Involvement

So what other rewards are possible? How about the opportunity to impact the quality of the workplace or the final product or service offered? As noted earlier, the opportunity to contribute useful ideas— employee involvement—is part of the *interactive phase* of employee development. Employee involvement of this kind is cause for celebration because it signifies employee growth and value. This is a precious commodity.

Responsiveness to employee ideas is part of the business philosophy of total quality systems. In these systems, the people closest to the job are given credit for knowing best what needs to be done to improve process and quality. This is a beautiful theory. The flaw in it is that there frequently is resistance and neglect in following up on suggestions offered by employees. Employees perceive the lack of direct response as a sign that managers don't care about them or their ideas— even in those organizations that profess to believe in workforce involvement. Even the most well-intentioned supervisors don't provide enough praise. And, even the best supervisors do a poor job of updating employees on the progress of suggestions being considered. At this writing, few American businesses have matured to provide "self managed work teams" the authority to followup on their own ideas. Rather than "hallucinate," or think the worst, as immature employees frequently do when they don't see followup on their ideas, employees who have legitimately advanced to a second phase of employee development need to initiate self publicity and also followup. They need to remind supervisors of their initial involvement and continuing concern. Sometimes supervisors simply forget. Proactive communication encourages additional celebration by ensuring followup and potential rewards that go along with it. At any point where employees are still earning their credibility, initiation of followup is essential.

▼ Supervisory Recognition

Positive feedback is to be cherished, especially if it is honestly deserved. Genuine praise may even be compliments in departmental meetings and mentions in company newsletters, for instance. Enhanced self esteem is the result, and continued recognition increases the employee's referent and expert power.

▼ Integration into Informal Groups

Different research has concluded that integration into informal groups is the main source of employee satisfaction in organizations.[20] Integration means social acceptance. By contributing to the work and sharing the leadership, employees become an integral part of the group. In so doing, they feel satisfaction and reduce certain kinds of stress.[21] Group acceptance provides a support system for behavioral and mental wellbeing. It also develops personal respect and popularity. These dynamics increase future influence in the workplace. They also lead to friendships that extend beyond the job.

Summary of Celebration: *Interactive Phase*

- ✔ Material reward in the form of pay increases and bonuses.
- ✔ Training and development.
- ✔ Employee involvement and empowerment, contribution to the quality of work life, followup.
- ✔ Supervisory recognition.
- ✔ Integration into informal groups, respect, personal satisfaction, peer relationships.

Summary: *Interactive* Maturity
and Empowerment Opportunities

Most people want to do a good job and want to have an impact on their work environment. John Young, president of Hewlett Packard, attempted to convince his supervisors of this by telling them to give people a job and the information necessary to do it, and they'll seldom be disappointed with employee performance. In this second phase of development, employees should be assessing constantly their job performance, important company decisions, roles in employee groups, and changes on the horizon. On a regular basis those employees should be contributing ideas to solve the problems besetting them and the organization. Finally, they should initiate followup and celebration. At the end of this chapter you will find some suggested targets for building skills and organizational perspective (Table 4).

Some employees have additional motivation. Gifford Pinchot suggests that the exceptional employees seek out opportunities to gain job-related freedom.[22] They continue to perform and offer solutions to day-to-day work problems. They also begin to search for creative ideas for significant improvement in organization performance or tasks not being accomplished that they may take on as their own. Listening, asking for more information concerning organizational needs and requirements, seeking reasons why, and observing behaviors and work flow are good mechanisms for assessing additional opportunities. Asking additional questions about overall company operation, particularly in terms of cost containment and customer needs, provides a broader knowledge base for understanding how and why to approach such opportunities. And more mature employees stay current with national and global conditions in their business.

Other benefits, including the discovery of intricacies of organizational functioning, career paths and development potential, and educational enhancement opportunities are very real. The result is increased control over the organizational environment, including greater influence on decisions, work freedom, and other opportunities beyond the requirements of the basic job.

Decision making and innovation are best facilitated with teamwork between supervisors and nonsupervisors. Contemporary business writers are calling for more "partnerships" between staff and management.[23] Open communication flow in all directions—upward, downward, and horizontally—is critical to the development of such partnerships. The responsibilities for keeping that communication open is also shared. What we have traditionally considered to be management responsibilities become shared to the extent that employees choose to have some personal control over their work life—control which they should be able to initiate if they are achieving their basic work requirements. When members of the management/worker team do not do what they are supposed to do, the other members must pick up the slack; when members close communication channels, hard feelings often result, while team unity and performance suffer.

While opportunities offered in this phase of development are stimulating and rewarding, achieving competencies characteristic of the *interactive phase* of development is also critical to "employability." Workers in this decade and beyond must have both technical and interpersonal skills. (Table 3 offers an array of behaviors representing these skills.) For employability, employees will apply these skills to achieve even greater workplace influence and credibility and move into a more elite circle of workers—those treated as respected and trusted "consultants" to organizational performance.

Jeff: Case Study in Empowerment Choices

At a small manufacturing plant, Jeff, a nonsupervisory employee with a two-year track record of good performance suggested to his supervisor that the company could save a lot of money by recycling the paper used in computer operations. The supervisor thought the idea was so good that he asked the employee to suggest it to top executives. Jeff presented his idea to the vice president of the division during the next open employee meeting on the plant floor. The VP wrote down the suggestion but did not identify the employee who made it. Later, top management decided to investigate the idea and eventually discovered that they could save several thousand dollars a year by recycling computer paper! Needless to say, they instituted a recycling procedure and reaped the projected financial benefits.

During the investigation, neither Jeff, nor his supervisor, nor top management had done any followup with each other. The vice president maintained that he had not gotten information yet, so he had nothing to report back to the employee. Jeff said he did not feel it was his place to ask if the company was advancing his suggestion, though he did wonder about it. The supervisor said: "After Jeff made the suggestion to top management, I was no longer involved. I forgot all about it." To add insult to injury, once the management team decided to institute the new policy, they could not identify who had the idea in the first place. Red-faced, management chose not to make any public announcement of the new recycling effort because it would be deemed an usurpation of an employee idea. Instead, they chose to wait for the employee to come and ask about the idea so they could identify who was responsible and reward him appropriately.

Word of the new policy and its monetary benefit to the organization spread informally through the plant. When Jeff heard of it, he was incensed. No matter that the idea was making money for the company; he was upset that he was not even afforded the courtesy of a thank you. He vowed never to share an idea again—and seriously considered leaving the company. For a few days his performance even suffered as he stewed internally about lack of respect. Only after sharing his frustration with a co-worker who was privy to details of the investigation and the management dilemma were the appropriate communicators matched. Only then could they celebrate. However, by then there were many wounds, some of which would be hard to heal.

TABLE 3
Employee Behaviors
Characteristic of the *Interactive Phase**

▼ Has complete job knowledge.

▼ Produces quality work consistently.

▼ Plans work effectively and seeks out meaningful tasks to fill slowdowns.

▼ Requires help only on major projects, not regular work.

▼ Performs consistently even when supervision is absent.

▼ Consistently follows policies and procedures; infrequent problems with work habits.

▼ Expresses interest in additional tasks.

▼ Understands decision making process and participates in discussions.

▼ Understands and applies data based problem solving tools to improve quality; identifies problems and offers suggestions and options without being asked.

▼ Inquires about "rationale" behind decisions and operations.

▼ Seeks out information about the company; customers, plans, key issues.

▼ Assists others without being asked; is sought out by some team members for appropriate assistance.

▼ Consistently displays "team oriented" behavior and cooperation.

▼ Points to accomplishment as well as effort when evaluating own work.

▼ Capable of monitoring and evaluating own performance; able to identify longer term career goals.

▼ Displays appropriate "customer relations" skills and sensitivities.

▼ Able to identify causes of personal stress; works at stress management.

☐ **Developmental Check:** Have you taken action to assure the consistency of task performance and application of interpersonal skills necessary to earn greater empowerment?

*Supervisors across the country tell us that these behaviors are signs employees have achieved "functional maturity," and have entered a phase of employee development where they will interact more responsibly with management and work teams, and be given greater work freedom.

TABLE 4
Building Skills and Organizational Perspective Improvement Targets for *Interactive Phase*

1. Problem solving.
2. Project planning.
3. Supportive communication skills.
4. Conflict management.
5. Group leadership skills.
6. Continuous improvement and total quality approaches.
7. Customer service skills.
8. Selling ideas and proposals to others.
9. Basic business/professional writing.
10. Personal computer basics.
11. Time management.
12. Stress management.
13. Career planning.

Suggested Readings

▼ Publications and materials regarding your specific business, competitors and the business environment.

▼ Davis Bothe, *Industrial Problem Solving Using Dot Star.* Northville, MI: International Quality Institute, 1990.

▼ Karl Albrecht and Lawrence Bradford, *The Service Advantage: How to Identify and Fulfill Customer Needs.* Homewood, IL: Business One Irwin, 1990.

▼ Allan Cohen and David Bradford, *Influence Without Authority.* NY: John Wiley and Sons, 1990.

▼ Albert Ellis, *How to Stubbornly Refuse to Make Yourself Miserable About Anything. Yes. Anything.* NY: Carol Publishing Group, 1990.

▼ Robert Kriegel and Louis Patten, *If It Ain't Broke, Break It.* NY: Warner Books, 1991.

▼ Peter Scholtes, *The Team Handbook.* Madison, WI: Joiner, 1990.

Endnotes Chapter 4

[1]Mark Curtin, "Saying Goodbye to the Sheep Factory," *Journal for Quality and Participation.* September, 1991, p. 68.

[2]R. Henry Migliore, "Improving Worker Productivity Through Communicating Knowledge of Work Results," *Human Resource Management,* Graduate School of Business, University of Michigan, Ann Arbor, Michigan, Summer, 1970, pp. 26–32; Thomas E. Becker and Richard J. Klimoski, "A Field Study of the Relationship Between the Organizational Feedback Environment and Performance," *Personnel Psychology,* Summer, 1989, pp. 343–358.

[3]Our own contractual research with for-profit and nonprofit organizations seldom turns up money as a key motivator for people. Anecdotal information from popular management magazines and our own experience further reinforces the conclusion. The original conclusion was offered by Frederick Herzberg, Bernard Mausner, and Barbara Synderman, *The Motivation to Work.* New York: John Wiley and Sons, Inc., 1959.

[4]Kenneth A. Kovach, "What Motivates Employees? Workers and Supervisors Give Different Answers,"*Business Horizons,* 1988, pp. 58–65.

[5]"Interview with Kenneth Blanchard," *ManagersEdge ANSWER LINE.* Englewood, Colorado: ManagersEdge Corporation, 1988.

[6]Daniel Katz and Robert L. Kahn, *The Social Psychology of Organizations.* New York: John Wiley and Sons, Inc., 1966.

[7]William L. Van Horn and William D. Stinnett, "The Ideal Work Environment: Total Employee Involvement," *S.A.M. Advanced Management Journal,* Autumn, 1984, pp. 41–45; Rick L. Lansing, The Power of Teams," *Supervisory Management,* February, 1989, pp. 39–43; Mitchell Lee Marks, Edward J. Hackett, Philip H. Mirvis, and James F. Grady, Jr., "Employee Participation in a Quality Circle Program: Impact on Quality of Work Life, Productivity, and Absenteeism," *Journal of Applied Psychology,* February, 1986, pp. 61–69.

[8]"Pocket Veto," *Elan Vital,* Denver, CO: Signature Resources, Spring, 1989, p. 2.

[9]Mary Ann Von Glinow, "Reward Strategies for Attracting, Evaluating, and Retaining Professionals," *Human Resource Management,* Summer, 1985, pp. 191–205.

[10]Dennis D. Phillips and Les Wallace, "Initiate Employee Input," *Personnel Journal,* February, 1988, pp. 22–23.

[11]*Labor-Management Cooperation: 1989 State-of-the-Art Symposium.* Washington, D.C.: U.S. Department of Labor Bureau of Labor-Management Relations and Cooperative Programs, 1989.

[12]Jack Orsburn, Linda Moran, Ed Musselwhite, and John Zenger, *Self Directed Work Teams.* Homewood, IL: Business One Irwin, 1990; Richard Wellins, William Byham, and Jeanne Wilson, *Empowered Teams.* San Francisco, Jossey Bass, 1991.

[13]Miriam Erez, P. Christopher Earley, and Charles L. Hulin, "The Impact of Participation on Goal Acceptance and Performance: A Two-Step Model," *Academy of Management Journal,* March, 1985, pp. 50–66; Van Horn and Stinnett; William J. Storch, "Participative Management Brings Employees into Problem Solving," *Chemical and Engineering News,* March 26, 1984, pp. 10–12.

[14]Teresa M. Harrison, "Communication and Participative Decision Making: An Exploratory Study," *Personnel Psychology,* Winter, 1985, pp. 93–116.

[15]Peter Scholtes, *The Team Handbook.* Madison, WI: Joiner Associates, 1990; Lawrence Miller and Jennifer Howard, *Managing Quality Through Teams.* Atlanta, GA: Miller Consulting Group, 1991.

[16]Gerald M. Goldhaber, Michael P. Yates, D. Thomas Porter, and Richard Lesniak, "Organizational Communication: 1978," *Human Communication Research,* Fall, 1978, pp. 76–96.

[17]Beverly Kaye and Kathryn McKee, "New Compensation Strategies for New Career Patterns," *Personnel Administrator,* March, 1986, p. 61.

[18]*P&QI: Productivity and Quality Improvement in the 90s,* The Results of the Ninth Productivity Survey Conducted by the Institute of Industrial Engineers.

[19]Herzberg; Joseph McKendrick, "Attendance," *Management World,* November, 1984; Lawrence S. Rothenberg, "Organizational Maintenance and the Retention Decision in Groups," *American Political Science Review,* December, 1988.

[20]Goldhaber, Yates, Porter, and Lesniak.

[21]Fredric M. Jablin, "Task/Work Relationships: A Life-Span Perspective," *Handbook of Interpersonal Communication,* M. L. Knapp and G. R. Miller (eds.). Beverly Hills, CA: Sage, 1985; "Does Job Satisfaction Prevent Back Injuries?" *Business Week,* April 1, 1991, p. 82.

[22]Gifford Pinchot III, *Intrepreneuring.* New York: Harper & Row, Publishers, 1985.

[23]Rosabeth Moss Kanter, *When Giants Learn to Dance.* New York: Simon and Schuster, 1989.

Chapter

Consultative Phase Maturity: Advanced Stages of Employee Development

"Things may come to those who wait,
but only the things left by those who hustle."
Abraham Lincoln

"Success is not the result of spontaneous combustion.
You must set yourself on fire."
Reggie Leach

Barreling down the Sixth Avenue freeway at rush hour, behold the student driver. Stuck in the center lane, slowed with sheepish grin and turn signal ablaze, hoping to get a break into another lane. Do the mature drivers blink? Heavens no. Let the poor kid fend for himself, it's a cruel world and we've got places to go and people to see. Traffic will clear by 9:30 and maybe he can merge then.

You've seen it on the road but do you also recognize it in the workplace? The co-worker needing a hand, struggling with a situation, project, or task, obviously in need of a break, behavioral turn signals flashing.

Most of us see this every day: phones ringing off the hook, customers piled up, struggling with a new assignment, confusion during a meeting, behind schedule on an important project, overloaded by a late assignment, cut off from communication by rude co-workers. Team work means pitching in. Invest each day in clarifying, assisting, and reaching out. We owe it to one another. A courtesy break in traffic won't sidetrack your trip. Team work means you too!

—"Student Driver." Reprinted from *Elan Vital*. Denver: Signature Resources, Fall, 1989.

An entrepreneur is a person who starts a business, takes risk, and is full of ideas. Gifford Pinchot III introduced the concept of the 'intrapreneur'' as an adaptation of the concept within already-existing organizations. He refers to an intrapreneur as a worker who takes personal responsibility for innovation and achievement—the ''dreamer who figures out how to turn an idea into a profitable reality.''[1]

Actualizing Personal Empowerment

In many ways this chapter is about intrapreneuring. It depicts the employee with a successful track record on basic tasks who has also contributed to improvement, innovation, and decision making within the organizational culture. This, the pinnacle of workplace achievement, is the stage in which the employee has considerable potential for autonomy and upward mobility. It is the stage in which personal credibility is highest. Unfortunately, it is a level of career maturity which some employees choose (either deliberately or subconsciously) not to attain.

Why would people limit their development? Perhaps some are comfortable knowing that they are performing satisfactorily and somewhat involved while allowing others to take the risks involved in leadership. Robert Schaffer, who has written about ''breakthrough performance'' factors, explains: '' . . . people establish invisible limits to the levels of achievement and change they feel able to reach, limits that are far short of potential. Within those limits loom uncertainty and anxiety.''[2] Many workers are satisfied with the levels of influence and challenge attained in the *interactive phase* of development. Thus, they choose to invest extra energy in interests outside of the workplace.

For others there is a perception that to do anything more means being asked continuously to do even more. And some supervisors may inhibit further employee development for fear of employees becoming threatening to their jobs. Other people frequently refuse to recognize or accept the opportunity for self-control in organizations. In the organizational psychology literature these people are frequently referred to as ''pawns.'' ''Since he feels that external factors determine his fate, the pawn does not consider carefully his goals in life, nor does he concern himself about what he himself can do to further his cause.''[3]

No matter. The truly exceptional workers—those who find opportunity in work as in play, those who see things as they might be, those who want to make a mark and use all the capabilities they can find—will enter the advanced phase regardless of real or imagined barriers. At this stage they can experiment and behave with greater freedom. They have the power and influence even though they may not have the authority of hierarchical position.[4] This phase is seen by many as the ultimate in work satisfaction. We call this level of attainment the *"consultative phase."* Supervisors treat employees at this level as peer consultants and count on them to tackle difficult issues of team leadership, problem solving, innovation, and change. Employees this mature are also frequently promoted to supervisory and management positions.

Expectations in Developing *Consultative* Maturity

The consultative phase is for exceptional people. While supervisors and upper level managers can facilitate employee advancement toward this level, employees must internalize the drive and want to meet the challenges and opportunities for self actualization.[5] The feelings of freedom and accomplishment that result from success at this stage are highly satisfying.[6]

▼ Freedom

Employees at this level of development should expect FREEDOM—freedom to "own" a project, complete with its responsibilities and consequences. They expect freedom to gain the self esteem that comes with demonstrating leadership regardless of their position in the organization.

While many progressive companies alter job assignments to allow time on pet projects, most employees at this level are not necessarily relieved of routine tasks.[7] Projects for which one gains responsibility need not be major in scope to be significant. They must only add value to the workplace.[8] Self empowered employees will always find the little things that make jobs easier and will accomplish them even if the blessings of the organization come only as an afterthought.

Two cautions are in order here. First, we are talking about intrapreneurial freedom—that is, freedom WITHIN THE STRUCTURE to develop creative ideas that benefit the organization and are personally enjoyable. Second, before such freedom can be expected, it must be earned—through performance excellence in the *instructive* and *interactive phases*.

▼ Modeling Behavior

Frequently, opportunity at this level is not formalized by project assignment or special request by supervisors. Opportunity may come from personal initiative. Opportunity may come simply from being a good example to others in team problem solving, staff meetings, or new employee orientation. Influence may come from being an informal leader of the work group to whom others come for advice. Empowered leadership means focusing task discussions, harmonizing conflict, and summarizing and taking consensus; in sum, it means demonstrating interpersonal competence. It is important to recognize that this phase may involve less visible opportunities and activities as well as more formal project assignments or promotions. In any case you will gain credibility through success—however small it may seem. Expect to be observed and emulated.

▼ Personal Involvement

At the *consultative phase* employees might receive less information on tasks and fewer responses to their performance. Some feedback is still essential for morale,[8] but personal achievement comes to have its own rewards. It's not that supervisors don't appreciate the quality of work; it's just that often they are so grateful to have one less person to worry about that they focus energies on other staff. Employees in this phase usually find plenty of personal satisfaction. At the same time they are not relieved of the need to perform—or of the need to get along with people. Indeed, co-workers frequently watch emerging leaders more closely when they have reached higher levels of credibility. Advancing workers need to be attentive to how their behavior affects the team's ability to function smoothly.

Summary of Expectations: *Consultative Phase*

✔ Freedom, in the context of intrapreneurial freedom, personally empowered to exert leadership.

✔ Modeling behavior including team expectations for leadership, realization of being more closely monitored by co-workers.

✔ Personal involvement, self monitoring, less direct day-to-day feedback, demonstration of interpersonal competence.

Responsibilities: The Roles of Communication

Initiative, achievement, and control are personal responsibilities of the empowered employee. When opportunities are not formally presented by the company, employees need to create them. They realize that it is easier to ask for forgiveness than for permission.

▼ Personal Initiative and Drive

Trustworthiness is a key element of credibility for the empowered employee. As noted earlier, competence is an on-going dimension of credibility, and personableness has been reflected in teamwork and networking. Now, it becomes essential to demonstrate the capacity to take on projects and see them through to completion. Personal motivation is imperative.

Motivation is internal. The employee seeks opportunity and task ownership. And employees at this level need to overcome obstacles. They should be diplomatic, but they should not take "no" for an answer. When opportunities are not formally presented by the company, self-directed employees will create them. This is not a formula for revolution, but a candid recognition that in less supportive organizations, empowerment involves some risk. Not all organizations are ready to deal with top achievers.

▼ Sustaining Basic Competence

Many employees have leaped into new opportunities and neglected their primary job—only to discover their freedom restricted and their credibility damaged. (Remember Darryl.) At any level of personal development, it is still performance as expected by the company that allows the firm to continue to achieve its goals and to continue to provide jobs. Overall competence is still the key to personal credibility.

▼ Continuous Improvement

Pressures on contemporary businesses for product and service quality necessitate continuous improvement.[10] And because performance expectations change in response to these pressures, even in the same job position, employees adapt to changing situations and help others do the same. Leaders anticipate product and service change and "act to preserve what is best and discard the rest."[11] All products and services have life cycles. They originate, change and require adaptation. Also, customer expectations are constantly changing. Continuous improvement, therefore, is not a management whim but instead a drive to survive.

▼ Shared Leadership

Shared leadership involves anticipating, adapting and acting within a context of "multiple constituents." As employees at this level of development expand their power and influence, they must still be sensitive to others. They may "own" a project, but they need to cooperate. Empathy and concern for people, and helping others achieve, are essential. In addition, shared leadership requires open communication with multiple constituents: keeping key people abreast of progress and achievement; and maintaining continuous interaction with management.

▼ Total Communication Perspective

The professionally mature employee must also be an effective listener. While some research suggests that listening is the skill deemed most important for the effective manager,[12] we believe that conclusion is as readily applied to the employees having earned job-related autonomy. The act of listening assures the greatest sensitivity to corporate climate. This involves a continual process of asking, clarifying, contributing ideas, and even voicing discontent when it is warranted— accompanied, of course, by constructive recommendations.

Supportiveness allows the advanced employee to continue to build bridges and develop the capacity of others. Even "owned" projects require the support and assistance of peers, if not of supervisors.

Timely sharing of information is crucial. Supervisors appreciate regular updates of progress, despite the level of autonomy they may have approved. Information sharing not only ensures the continued support of key personnel such as supervisors and departmental opinion leaders, it also builds the confidence of team members.

Finally, the astute employee will realize the value of oral briefings and public speaking skills. Most students required to take a course in basic public speaking in college argue that they will never use the skills, because they cannot foresee that they will ever speak in front of groups. When they enter the workforce, they find that selling ideas, representing their department in product line reviews, and instructing customers in the use of products become part of the myriad of speaking opportunities characteristic of empowerment and leadership.

Summary of Responsibility: *Consultative Phase*

✔ Personal initiative and drive, motivation.
✔ Basic competence.
✔ Continuous improvement.
✔ Shared leadership, sensitivity to team and organizational needs.
✔ Total communication perspective.

Celebration

Abraham Maslow labeled the highest level of his hierarchy of needs "self actualization." [13] *Celebration at the consultative phase of employee development should be thought of in the same way. The ultimate reward is personal freedom, and the celebration is internalized as self esteem and personal pride. The individual's own recognition of achievement supersedes all other rewards. It is, as the Army ad campaign reminds us, "being all that we can be."*

▼ Personal Self Esteem

At this level of advancement, personal self esteem may be the most important form of celebration.[14] The excitement of challenging work and the pride that comes with completion of an "owned" task are rewarding. They also motivate others. Additional freedom for other tasks becomes a possibility along with a corresponding power base and prestige—even in a nonsupervisory role. The system of rewards for highly innovative or influential people does not necessarily involve money or promotion. It involves latitude to apply experience to new situations, to take risks, and to invest the company's money in new ideas.[15]

▼ Position Change

Top-performing employees may also be rewarded with new positions. These can include mentorships, with accompanying opportunity to share wisdom, advancement within the organization, or movement into other challenging positions outside the organization.

Before accepting promotions, however, employees need to consider their own capacities and desires. For many, the reward is in the work, as hard as that may sound to the person currently crying out for financial reward. Recognize that promotion to supervision changes the formula for success. The new situation may lessen the motivation felt with previous responsibilities.

▼ Financial Compensation

While money may not be the prime motivator for advanced employees, the lack of financial recognition for performance can be discouraging.[16] Employees should feel that they are receiving fair and competitive compensation. Indeed, advanced employees may themselves create new means of compensation. Up to now, innovative compensation plans have come from the top down.[17] However, the phenomenon of team-influenced reward systems is becoming more common. When approaching management with ideas about monetary compensation, employees must be extremely diplomatic.

Whatever the celebration, the opportunities are likely to grow greater as the track record reflects successes.

Summary of Celebration: *Consultative Phase*

✔ Personal self esteem and freedom.
✔ Position change and mentorships.
✔ Project compensation and team-based rewards.

Summary of *Consultative Phase*

Personally empowered employees should be aware of trends, both within the organization and outside it. They should be prepared to deal with a changing workforce, including one that is becoming more culturally diverse. Sensitivity to roles, customers, and possible language barriers will help high-achieving workers go even farther.[18] At the end of this chapter you will find a list of behaviors characteristic of this phase (Table 5) and some suggested targets for building skills and organizational perspective (Table 6).

Self evaluation, an important task at any step of organizational progression, becomes especially critical when new opportunities lead to major changes in circumstance. Employees need to consider work and life priorities in making decisions. The fact that they have earned advancement should not render joy of work and personal motivation as unimportant. Quality of work life, quality of family life, and the quality of life in general, weighted against potential financial gain, become important considerations in assessing new opportunities.

Some employees, considering the full progression of organizational advancement, will argue that there is not time for assuming projects beyond the basic job requirements. They may say others are being paid to handle special projects and make decisions. To us such attitudes indicate that a person has not advanced to the *consultative phase*—and may not want to.

Somehow, there is always time for the achievement motivated individual—the one who understands organizational dynamics—to achieve and excel. When they are creating their own opportunities, the work becomes fun, rather than drudgery for the sake of survival. Every employee ought to ask where he or she wants to be and how his or her behaviors measure up. Personal development in organizations just might lead to greater quality and productivity of American organizations. The stories of Georgina, Larry, and Marcia will illustrate.

Case Studies in Personal Empowerment and Achievement

Georgina

To help pay her way through college, Georgina began working as a receptionist in a manufacturing plant. As she studied and worked, she developed a keen interest in the business and in the overall industry. Her work was simple and unchallenging, but Georgina used her contact with people in the plant to learn as much as she could about the business. She let her boss and others know that, though she had not finished college, she would be interested in considering a move closer to the ''action of the shop floor'' and would take time out from college to commit herself full time to a reasonable position.

Georgina's work and interpersonal relations were always of high caliber and her boss knew she could learn other jobs quickly. Without other experience, however, Georgina was not taken seriously by other supervisors in the plant. Instead of giving up, she volunteered for shopwide committee assignments (from trivial to significant) and used creative power and energy to get noticed. On the personnel committee, she showed a knack for dealing with sticky situations in a positive and upbeat manner and caught the eye of the division manager in metal fabrication. They talked some about her interests, and he kidded her about supervising on the shop floor in a tough manufacturing environment. Georgina continued to glean as much working knowledge as she could about the business and took courses that focused on supervisory skills and psychology. When a supervisory job opened up in welding, she indicated her interest. Although many felt she was kidding, Georgina was serious. Because of her committee experience, her knowledge in the business, and her reasoned appeal to be given a chance, she got the job.

Knowing virtually nothing about welding and having no direct supervisory experience, Georgina realized she was stretching herself. The work team took a while to get used to having a woman supervisor. But Georgina stuck with it. She soon developed a reputation of being fair, knowledgeable, and willing to get her hands dirty. She was a solution-oriented thinker. Her manager was somewhat surprised with the progress she made in a short time, but knew he didn't have to worry because Georgina kept him fully informed, sought advice and information, and rehearsed the handling of difficult employee issues with him. After about six months he said: "She didn't let me worry about how she was doing; she let me know on a regular basis. She wasn't afraid to say 'I don't know' and seek input from me or her employees. And her knowledge of the business as a whole was communicated to her staff resulting in significant improvements in quality and productivity."

After several years in the job, Georgina had significantly reduced production time, upgraded quality, become an advocate for interdepartmental cooperation, and was well respected throughout the plant as a leader. When the manager position for her division became vacant, the outgoing boss recommended her for the job. "She was ready," he said. "She had learned the job and the business backward and forward. She displayed an ability to learn new skills quickly. Despite dropping out of college, she had taken every opportunity to take workshops locally to learn new skills and stay introduced to new ideas. I knew this management position would be a stretch initially and that some employees would be difficult, but this woman was a self starter who could be trusted and the right one for the job."

Georgina accepted the position despite some self doubts about her ability to handle something that big. While she struggled with some "old buffaloes" who resisted a woman with such authority in the manufacturing environment, the style and credibility she displayed in her other assignments shines through in her new position. Georgina is now partly responsible for getting the company's CEO to establish a Total Quality Program. Despite misgivings about her abilities, she has taken faculty training to "train" other leaders and staff in TQM and is gaining confidence first by team teaching. While she still struggles with a few top administrators who try to run roughshod over her from time to time, she has proven to be a worthy advocate for the business, her division, and employees who work with her. To expand her horizons even further, Georgina is taking new courses on finance and budget as well as continuous quality improvement.

Did Georgina invest in learning the business, making internal contact, and publicizing her interests? Did Georgina commit to continued learning to upgrade her skills and knowledge? Did Georgina overcome her lack of position to learn and become noticed? Did Georgina stretch and challenge her own competencies? You bet she did.

Larry

Larry supervises the occupational therapy department of a suburban hospital. Having been with the hospital for nearly five years, he was promoted to this position because he is an excellent therapist and has a track record of providing innovative, yet inexpensive, ideas. In his current position, he went back to school part-time and nights to complete a master's degree in occupational therapy with support courses in communication, saying it would help him in his supervisory position.

Larry's master's thesis has been accepted for publication, and he is now working on another article. He insists on a quick one-to-one meeting with his supervisor at least once a week to tell of his accomplishments of weekly goals, his progress toward yearly goals, and plans for the future. Larry is a *consultative phase* employee who reflects motivation, maturity, and responsibility for accomplishment of organizational objectives. In fact, it appears that he has aligned his personal objectives with organizational goals. The accomplishment of one results in a positive reflection on the other.

After publication of his article, he received some publicity and travel support. He has requested additional travel support for further outreach. Indeed, he is submitting his third request since the first two were rebuffed. He promises to continue trying, never taking "no" for an answer. He expects to receive freedom and opportunity; he has gotten some and will get more; he has earned it.

Marcia

Marcia worked as a bank teller while majoring in business at the university. She mastered the basics quickly—to the point of becoming "a little bored" with the work. However, she appreciated the efforts of her bosses who accommodated her schedule by allowing time for classes and studying. She also appreciated the money. It gave her the opportunity to go to school in the first place. Her needs were being met, and she understood the tradeoffs.

Marcia worked consistently with a smile and became a favorite of bank personnel. Some even began to take advantage of her cooperative disposition. They often asked for help. Seldom did Marcia refuse, but when she did, she gave good reasons, and other employees appreciated her honesty. Marcia got a good, but not great, performance review at the end of her first year on the job. She was disappointed. "I really thought I was doing a great job," she said. "Nobody works harder. I try to be friendly and upbeat with customers all the time, and I really think I help other employees beyond the call of duty. But I gotta tell you. I have also been disappointed that I have not gotten recognition as a 'spirit award' winner at any time through the year. Maybe I really am doing something wrong." [Spirit award refers to an award similar to employee of the month at other organizations. It requires nomination by a fellow employee or customer and then supervisory agreement.]

After reflecting upon the review, Marcia asked her supervisor to explain each area of weakness and what specifically she could do to improve. (She had to ask three or four times and then arrange a special appointment with the supervisor.) Once that was done to her satisfaction, Marcia was determined to improve in areas where she did not receive an outstanding rating.

A number of things happened during her second year of work. She received the "spirit award" twice. She was recognized by her immediate supervisor once for outstanding performance and another time for teamwork by the loan supervisor. She asked for and received responsibility for scheduling all part-time tellers. As a result she can now accommodate not only her school schedule but also her play schedule. She is still popular. She is still asked to do extra work by other employees, and she still does most of it willingly. Is she overworked? At one point in her development, she said this: "Basically, I like my job, and I especially like the people I work with. But I'm still a part-time employee with no opportunity (yet) for management. So what could I do? I could mope through regular work hours, do the basic stuff, do an average job, and be bored. Or I could suck up some pride, work on where the supervisor thought I was weak, assume some other duties, and demonstrate I was a hotshot. I took the second choice, and I like it. Do I work too hard? Probably, by some people's standards. But my work days go fast. And I challenge myself to be the best at what I do even if it's at the bottom of the organization. You know, I've made it pretty fun, and I'll remember this when I'm a manager somewhere.''

With yet a year and a half to go in college, Marcia was promoted, then offered a lateral move in the company. At this writing, she is considering the substantial monetary gain and security to be attained by staying on after graduation. The organization has offered her that opportunity.

TABLE 5
Behavioral Characteristics of the Consultative Phase of Empowerment*

▼ Consistently exceeds performance expectations in both quality and quantity.

▼ Plans work thoroughly; sees both near and long term objectives.

▼ Identifies work improvements; evaluates options and benefits.

▼ Anticipates change and continuously improves.

▼ Sees the "big picture" organizationally and broader business environment.

▼ Assists others without being asked; acts as coach.

▼ Source of work information for team and others.

▼ Accepts independent responsibility; self empowered.

▼ Participates in decision making and problem solving discussions.

▼ Provides clear leadership in team discussion and management of team relationships.

▼ Self assesses professional development needs and acts on them independently.

▼ Develops long term career plans.

▼ Maintains even disposition through effective stress management.

▼ Assertively and responsibly represents team and workplace issues to management and others.

▼ Interpersonally competent.

☐ **Development Check:** Have you accepted responsibility to act as a trusted consultant to your team and organization? Is your behavior consistent with the highest level of personal and professional credibility?

*Supervisors across the country tell us these behaviors are highly respected and result in greater autonomy and leadership.

TABLE 6
Building Skills and Organizational Perspective Improvement Targets for *Consultative Phase*

1. Team building.
2. Chairing meetings.
3. Negotiation and conflict management skills.
4. Orientation and training skills.
5. Coaching and reinforcing peer worker accomplishment.
6. Briefing/presentation skills.
7. Project management.
8. Supervision and leadership.
9. Strategic planning.
10. Decision making.
11. Change management and communication.
12. Organizational behavior.
13. Proposal and report writing.
14. "Total Quality" and "Continuous Improvement" theory and practice.
15. Managing multiple demands.
16. Leading culturally diverse work teams.

Suggested Readings

▼ Publications regarding the business environment and management.

▼ James Belasco, *Teaching the Elephant to Dance: Empowering Change in Your Organization*. NY: Crown Publishers, 1990.

▼ Max DePree, *Leadership Is An Art*. NY: Doubleday, 1987.

▼ Roger Fisher and William Ury, *Getting to Yes: Negotiating Agreement Without Giving In*. NY: Penguin Books, 1985.

▼ Rosabeth Moss Kanter, *The Changemasters*. NY: Simon and Schuster, 1983.

▼ Dennis Kinlaw, *Coaching For Commitment*. San Diego: University Associates, 1989.

▼ Otto Kroeger and Janet Thuesen. *Type Talk at Work: How the 16 Personality Types Determine Your Success on the Job*. NY: Delacorte Press, 1992.

▼ Jack Orsburn, Linda Moran, Ed Musselwhite and John Zenger, *Self Directed Work Teams: The New American Challenge*. Homewood, IL: Business One Irwin, 1990.

Endnotes Chapter 5

[1]Robert Schaffer, "Results Improvement Is the Key to Creativity and Empowerment," *Journal for Quality and Participation*, September, 1991, p. 20.

[2]Gifford Pinchot III, *Intrapreneuring*. New York: Harper & Row, Publishers, 1985, p. ix.

[3]Richard DeCharms, "From Pawns to Origins: Toward Self-Motivation," *Psychology and Educational Practice*, Gerald S. Lesser (ed.). Glenview, IL: Scott, Foresman, 1971, pp. 381–382.

[4]Allan R. Cohen and David L. Bradford, *Influence without Authority*. New York: John Wiley & Sons, 1990.

[5]William Schutz, *The Interpersonal Underworld*. Palo Alto, California: Science and Behavior Books, 1966. Abraham H. Maslow, *Motivation and Personality*. New York: Harper & Row, Publishers, 1954.

[6]David B. Greenberger, Stephen Strasser, Cummings, and Dunham, "The Impact of Personal Control on Performance and Satisfaction," *Organizational Behavior and Human Decision Processes*, pp. 29–48.

[7]"Farewell Fast Track." *Business Week*, December 12, 1990, pp. 192–200.

[8]Greg R. Oldam and Christina E. Shalley, "Effects of Goal Difficulty and Expected External Evaluation on Intrinsic Motivation," *Academy of Management Journal*. September, 1985, pp. 628–640.

[9]Rick L. Lansing, "The Power of Teams," *Supervisory Management*, February, 1989, pp. 39–43.

[10]See for example, J. M. Juran, *Juran on Planning for Quality*. New York: The Free Press, 1988; Karl Albrecht, *At America's Service*. Homewood, Illinois, Dow Jones-Irwin, 1988; Masaaki Imai, *Kaizen*, Random House, 1986.

[11]Charles Garfield, *Peak Performers*. New York: Avon Books, 1986.

[12]Samual L. Becker and Leah R. V. Ekdom, "The Forgotten Basic Skill: Oral Communication," *Association for Communication Administration Bulletin*, 1980, pp. 12–25.

[13]Maslow.

[14]Lawrence S. Rothenberg, "Organizational Maintenance and the Retention Decision in Groups," *American Political Science Review*, December, 1988, p. 1131.

[15]Vijay Sathe, "From Surface to Deep Corporate Entrepreneurship," *Human Resource Management*, Winter, 1988, pp. 389–411.

[16]Frederick Herzberg, Bernard Mausner, and Barbara Synderman, *The Motivation to Work*. New York: John Wiley and Sons, Inc., 1959.

[17]"Here Come Richer, Riskier Pay Plans," *Fortune*, December 19, 1988, pp. 50–58.

[18]William B. Johnston and Arnold H. Packer, *Workforce 2000*. Indianapolis, Indiana: Hudson Institute, June, 1987; see also, Marilyn Loden and Judy Rosener, *Workforce America: Managing Employee Diversity as a Vital Resource*. Homewood, IL: Business One Irwin, 1991.

6

Organizational Politics

Any text on this topic would be incomplete without a discussion of organizational "politics." Even when behaving appropriately, employees are never guaranteed anticipated rewards, benefits, or promotions. While many companies and organizations advertise their commitment to "excellence" and say they are "customer driven" and "world class," this can be nothing more than "CEO babble."[1] We can control our own behaviors. We cannot control the behaviors of others. Recognition of this reality early in one's work career helps prevent frustration. Many researchers have tried to explain why advancement and reward do not always result from merit, diligence, hard work, and doing things "the right way." Here are some reasons why.[2]

Political Realities

▼ Our personal influence may increase as we are seen by those in power to be like themselves. In other words, behaving like the boss can lead to greater trust from the boss. People who emulate the powerful managerial echelon tend to be thought of in a positive light. This can cast work-related competence into at least partial irrelevance. And it may explain, in part, why mid-level supervisors tend to develop managerial styles similar to those of their bosses; the political consequence in some organizations is advancement. If you work in an autocratic environment, your personal empowerment may take a longer and more subtle track.

▼ Power holders have advantages over others in at least two ways. Those who have superior knowledge and skill exert personal power. But there is also power of position. Those who hold higher positions are stronger even though they may be no greater in knowledge or skill than those who work under them. Personally insecure power holders often disregard subordinate achievers in order to avoid the potential threat to their influence and control. Levels of maturity in dealing with power and influence differ from person to person.

▼   It is frequently difficult to separate "individual" performance from successful "team performance." The really competent project worker may not receive individual recognition because the contribution is not clearly delineated from the overall performance of the team.

▼   Sometimes we believe we are better than we really are. Many employees overestimate their value to an organization. This, too, leads to frustration.

▼   Even when performance can be measured objectively, somebody in a power position must know about it and recognize it. That may not happen as frequently as we would like.

So you can't really avoid personal politics. But you can disagree with diplomacy, be persuasive, and maintain your own style and integrity in the swirl of competing personalities. In what follows we will show you how.

Disagreeing with Diplomacy

If you read major American business magazines, you know that every few years one of them focuses on "America's Toughest Bosses."[3] In almost any of those features, you will find quotations by staff that indicate the career risk involved in "disagreeing with the boss." If you pick up a sampling of other business and professional magazines, you also find stories and articles detailing the difficulty of expressing disagreement and minority opinion in problem solving groups, or with colleagues who are "difficult." Why do we see all this attention to the subject? Because many people react to the expression of different opinions and ideas as if they were personal attacks. Indeed, sometimes they are! But even when not meant to be, or even when our confidence level can handle such disagreement, we have learned that not all people are mature enough to handle differences of opinion without being defensive. Immature people tend to label every disagreement as a chink in their self esteem.

How do skilled communicators allow for the airing out of ideas and diverse points of view while protecting the dignity and self esteem of others? How do they press their points while minimizing hostility or alienation of others? They constantly modify their communication style and language, and they watch *what* they say.

▼ Communication Style

Learn to withhold judgment. Hold that quick trigger that wants to blurt out, ''I disagree.'' Early judgments provoke unnecessary antagonism. Demonstrate good listening skills and sincere interest in getting the facts and full picture. Assure others that you understand the ''whys'' and ''wherefores'' of their position, including the data (or lack of) upon which they base their case. Even then, consider whether your disagreement is that important. Choosing your conflicts wisely keeps you from wading into difficult situations that didn't really matter.

When you must disagree, try to find areas of commonality or agreement to emphasize. Building upon agreement, however minor, shows that you want to be cooperative rather than antagonistic. Few adversaries are a full 180° apart. Common ground can be found in most disagreements. Also remember to reinforce good points made by others. Give compliments.

When disagreeing, also work to maintain a respectful tone of voice so that it matches the supportive language and style you're attempting to develop. Review sections in Chapter 2 that deal with supportive communication and conflict management.

▼ Less Confrontational Language

You must also avoid using confrontational language. Don't make the disagreement personal. Speak to the facts. Focus on the problem. Dig at the facts as a means of jointly uncovering faulty perceptions.

Instead of personalized phrases like ''you don't understand'' or ''you're making a mistake here,'' use expressions like ''my experiences have been different'' or ''I view that information from a different angle.'' Or ''I'm not sure I've gotten all the facts yet. Can you give me a specific example of that problem?'' Or, ''Have we double checked that?''

Differences of opinion and perception are frequently based upon mistaken information. Your language can express concern about how you see the facts and perceive the objectives differently, while keeping what you say from being taken as personal accusations. Seeking to discover how such differences may have come about, and giving the other person room to back up, shift, or recognize ambiguity may save you a frontal attack on their position. Then again, you may need to reconsider your own position. You need to show you are willing to do that.

When you must confront distinct differences of opinion, use language that indicates your regard for the person. For example, ''I can respect your perception of the issues. I simply see it differently and here's why.'' Or, ''I'm not comfortable yet with the same conclusions based on that information.'' Whatever you say, always give your reasons for disagreeing succinctly and without suggesting that you are smarter than anyone else.

When you feel alternative ideas or solutions must be explored and may even be preferable to what someone else has suggested, again, adopt language that poses your issues and concerns less frontally, yet gets them put on the table. For example, ''What about this alternative?'' Does this have a bearing on what we're looking at?'' ''Could we look at XYZ?''

Such tentative approaches may lead people to consider your ideas more easily than directly stating that you don't agree. These alternatives won't always work, but they will improve many situations when applied consistently.

When direct confrontation is unavoidable use language that puts the weight on your own perception, rather than accusing the other person of being wrong. For example, ''Jack I'm concerned that we're overlooking the significance of idea X, and I need to get that in the record.'' ''Martha, I really need you to know that I don't think this is a good idea. I'm not challenging your authority or judgment, but want you to hear that I'm still not convinced.'' Or maybe, ''I need your help, Bill. Let's make sure we're both not overlooking something here. Would a second look or second opinion be worth the investment?''

Statements like these put you on record, yet don't aggressively challenge the authority or integrity of the other people, especially if they are your supervisors in the organization.

▼ Communication Content

While language and style help reduce defensive reactions, you must also make sure you do your homework when presenting a different opinion. Always be prepared to deal in solutions. It's not considered acceptable, in any arena, simply to criticize without having other ideas or additional information to put into the discussion. It helps to relate your ideas and alternatives directly to the broader solutions or preferred scenarios being sought by your peer or boss. Ideas are accepted more easily that way, and all our ideas must compete in the marketplace of alternatives. Additionally, make your objections and suggestions as concrete as possible. Be specific and use specific examples. Abstract ideas and concerns are less likely to receive attention unless you can support your case with real-world alternatives and data.

What about times when you blow it, when the quick trigger or personal accusation creeps into your relationships? Behave like a professional—just as you would want others to behave. Good communicators are not perfect. They simply catch themselves and correct more frequently than others. Call a time out, admit you got off on the wrong foot. Acknowledge that you were attacking the person rather than the problem. Professionals are able to control their emotions, think on their feet and demonstrate the skills and strategies we've discussed. When you have to go on record as opposed, you'll find a more cooperative response to your ideas and less defensiveness if you keep these principles in mind.

Selling Ideas and Proposals to Bosses and Others

The success of any idea or suggestion is related to the extent to which it has a solid impact. In other words, how well are we able to sell it in the arena of competing ideas and proposals? Few of us have escaped the frustration of having our good ideas hit a stone wall of resistance or disinterest. The reality is that many of those walls won't come down even if our ideas are the greatest. The good news is that we can maximize our chances of influencing work groups, our bosses and entire organizations by following a few simple guidelines. We encourage you to consider four major areas where a little forethought and preparation will pay off.

▼ Organizational Goals and Objectives

Your chances of selling an idea are enhanced the more you relate it to the achievement of shared objectives. Many organizations openly discuss these; others do not. Your homework begins in determining what your organization has decided is important and finding ways in which your idea will advance its work. If you're uncertain, ask your supervisor for clarification. If that gets you nowhere, you may have to do your best detective work, draw conclusions based upon direct observation of how systems work in your organization, then take your chances. If you're in a progressive organization where goals and objectives are fairly common knowledge, you have a sales advantage. If not, you've got work to do.

▼ Key Questions of Management

Here's where you must do the most preparation. Well conceived ideas are sold based upon the answer to four critical management questions:

1. How does the idea impact quality of products or services delivered?

2. How does the idea relate to profitability? Specifically, does it cut costs, generate greater revenue, or improve pricing in the marketplace? If so, how?

3. How does the idea impact people? Does it foster a pleasant and safe working environment? Does it help other departments and employees? Does it provide job enrichment?

4. What are the consequences if the organization does not implement your idea?

These are the questions your boss will ask, and they will be asked by his or her boss as ideas filter up the organizational hierarchy. Find out as much as you can about what the customers (internal and external) want and what they currently think about your product or service. Quality is what the customer says it is. Relate your suggestions directly to these customer expectations.

While you may not be a cost accounting specialist and able to develop a detailed financial *pro forma* for your idea, you will increase your chances of success by generally considering how cost containment and profitability are involved. We find that most people can think through these concepts very well and co-workers can even provide rough calculations based upon gross dollar figures. Whatever your sophistication, grapple with these key management questions to refine your proposal.

▼ Pilot Testing

Most people prefer to take risks in small increments. Whatever your ideas, consider how they might be tested with minimal risk. Is there a particular customer group, section of manufacturing, area of the office, work team or project which might pilot your concept? Can you break your idea down into small adjustments that can be made to current systems? Continuous improvement involves lots of minor alterations over time. Such an approach may be easier to sell. If you're willing to have your idea judged on results, this is a great way to leverage support.

▼ Pressure Points

While most of us would like to think we make decisions rationally, we cannot overlook the role of self interest and emotion in the process. Bosses are no different. They have pressures, biases, and soft spots. Learn them, observe them, and express yourself with these factors in mind. Reducing frustration, looking good with top management, improving working relationships may all play as important a role in selling your idea as profit. Look for and try to understand the pressures your boss feels and incorporate those into your pitch. Most of the time your appeals to profitability, quality and work environment will highlight your boss' key concerns.

Is it possible to sell a bad idea based solely upon a boss' emotion or biases? Yes. If that's the only way you can influence an organization, then you'll have to be your own conscience. For most of us, however, doing our homework properly provides a rewarding degree of influence, and it leaves professional integrity intact.

Even if your ideas don't consistently win in the organizational arena as frequently as your would like, by following these strategies you at least will be seen as a mature decision maker willing to have your ideas evaluated in the bright light of business reality. That makes you a winner in the estimation of most people.

Maintaining a Personal Style and Identity Within the Organizational Culture

All employees will have their integrity, self control, and confidence challenged throughout their work lives. The politics of groups assures that some co-workers will tempt you to cut corners, blur ethical boundaries, or just plain lie. For example, although we identified "admitting mistakes" as a behavior that may enhance credibility, owning up to mistakes requires considerable confidence and character. Not all members of your work group may encourage or support such behavior from you, especially if your admission reflects adversely upon others in the group. No matter how supportive or cooperative you are, your strength of character will threaten someone.

▼ Work Group Pressure.

In any work group there are also those who encourage us to limit productivity and maintain minimal performance standards so that the group as a whole won't be called upon to work harder. Psychological research recognizes that work group pressure can be severe and difficult to resist.[4] Recognize that making an individual choice about performance and effort is not as simple as it may sound.

Other work group pressures may compromise employee integrity. During your career you will observe employees who file misleading reports, withhold information, shade information, and develop many ways to favor their work group. When confronted with this, you may find it easier to back away from integrity. Ostracism, lack of cooperation, and outright hostility may be used to persuade you to be unethical or dishonest—or to condone that in the conduct of others. Often the difficult choice is whether to remain in the job and go along, or take a stand and possibly consider work elsewhere. While these choices can be made difficult through intimidation by other employees, we believe, and have consistently observed during 20 years of professional consulting experience, that maintaining your integrity results in long term career opportunity and success. Simply recognize, as do we, that such a choice may force short term difficulty and stress. Good people do win in the long run, however.

▼ You're In Control.

We control our behavioral choices. Consider the example we have all endured whatever our life or work history: the person who has ruined our day through inappropriate behavior, lack of cooperation or disparaging remarks. When we ask people in our training workshops how many have had someone ruin their day, every hand in the room goes up. When we ask how many people had permission to ruin their day, no hands go up. This lesson is critical to dealing with work politics and daily realities. Constant vigilance is required. Choose the positive behavior and recognize that reacting to the inappropriate behavior of others, intentional or not, most frequently leads to bigger problems and conflicts. Remind yourself that you lose advantage to manage the situation when you lose control over your reaction. When you choose the less mature behavior as a reaction to others or problems, you risk losing credibility. Maintaining self control requires extra effort. However, it is made easier by reminding yourself that empowerment and influence in the workplace depend upon how others evaluate your credibility.

Conclusion: Interpersonal Leadership and Empowerment

Those who know their job and do it well, and who also communicate effectively, are not guaranteed advancement and success. However, poor or mediocre workers, and those who can't communicate, will probably fail. The trends of the 1990's underscore this conclusion. Organizations are moving toward more people oriented work environments, emphasizing teamwork, quality focus, diversity, interpersonal competencies, and lifelong learning.

Successful employees of this and future decades will earn credibility through job skills AND skills in communication, problem solving, and leadership.[5] The successful career of the 1990's will be built on referent and expert power rather than traditional position or legitimate power. Commenting on this evolution in the workplace and its impact on workers at all levels, one author has said that new American workers ". . . must learn to operate without the might of the hierarchy behind them. The crutch of authority must be thrown away and replaced by their own personal ability to make relationships, use influence, and work with others to achieve results"[6]—in short, personal empowerment.

This book has been about self assessment, reality testing and focused work efforts, and about developing talents and recognizing leadership potential. It has also been about the important role which communication plays in job satisfaction and career success. Employees who choose to see themselves as "pawns" in the work scheme will view our approach as useless and frustrating. Those who recognize their capacity to learn and adapt and who accept responsibility for their own growth will find our suggestions energizing.

Endnotes Chapter 6

[1]Homer Johnson, "How to Secretly Start The Quality Revolution in Your Company," *Journal of Quality and Participation,* September, 1991, p. 90.

[2]For an extensive discussion of realities in contrast to ideal states or "myths," see: Gunnar Westerlund and Sven-Erik Sjostrand, *Organizational Myths.* New York: Harper & Row, Publishers, 1979.

[3]"America's Toughest Bosses," *Fortune,* February 27, 1989, pp. 40–54.

[4]Solomon Asch, "Opinions and Social Pressure," *Scientific American,* November, 1955, pp. 31–35; see also research summary regarding group conformity in M. E. Shaw, *Group Dynamics: The Psychology of Small Group Behavior.* New York: McGraw-Hill, 1981.

[5]Robert Levering, *A Great Place To Work.* New York: Random House, 1988; Karl Albrecht, *The Creative Corporation.* Homewood, IL: Dow Jones; Irwin, 1987.

[6]Rosabeth Moss Kanter, *When Giants Learn to Dance.* New York: Simon and Schuster, 1989, p. 361.

Index

Energize Your Organization, Employees and Management

With Practical Programs And Services From Signature Resources, Please Indicate Areas Of Interest And Return This Form

Professional Development and Organizational Consulting Services

- ❏ **APEALS**™: Talk To Your Doctor
- ❏ Appraisals: Staff and Management
- ❏ Attitude-Opinion Surveys
- ❏ Board of Directors Development
- ❏ Change: Anticipating and Managing
- ❏ Coaching Work Performance
- ❏ Collaborative Management Skills/Systems
- ❏ Communication Skills
- ❏ Community and Public Relations
- ❏ Conference Planning
- ❏ Corporate Culture: Assessment & Changes
- ❏ Corporate Credibility Enhancement
- ❏ Conflict Management
- ❏ Corporate Culture: Designing and Assessing
- ❏ Customer Relations:
  PEOPLE FIRST: Customer Relations CPR™
- ❏ Delegation
- ❏ Diversification Planning
- ❏ Employee Assistance Programs
- ❏ Employee Involvement Programs
- ❏ Employee Orientation Programs
- ❏ Executive Development
- ❏ Fundraising Strategies & Programs
- ❏ Health Care Systems and Programs
- ❏ Individualized Image and Skill Development
- ❏ Influence Without Authority
- ❏ Internal Communication Programs
- ❏ Interviewing Skills
- ❏ Leadership Styles and Skills Development
- ❏ Management Reorganization
- ❏ Managing Multiple Demands/Time Man.

- ❏ Managing Your Boss
- ❏ Market Based Planning
- ❏ Marketing Skills and Strategies
- ❏ Media Relations: Strategies and Skills
- ❏ Meetings: Management and Leadership
- ❏ Motivation: Individuals and Teams
- ❏ Negotiation Skills and Strategies
- ❏ Newsletter Development and Review
- ❏ Occupational and Employee Health Programs
- ❏ Organizational Assessment and Review
- ❏ Participative Management Systems
- ❏ Performance Coaching and Appraisal
- ❏ Personal Productivity
- ❏ Personnel Selection
- ❏ Planning: Strategic and Operational
- ❏ Presentations:
  SPEAK WITH CREDIBILITY™
- ❏ Problem Solving Skill
- ❏ Productivity Programs
- ❏ Professional Credibility
- ❏ Professional Development Programs
- ❏ Project Team Management
- ❏ Recruitment and Retention
- ❏ Sales: Face to Face Marketing Skills
- ❏ Stress Management
- ❏ Succession Planning
- ❏ Supervision: Introductory and Advanced Skills
- ❏ Team Building/Self Managed Teams
- ❏ Team Leader/Project Leader Skills
- ❏ Training/Teaching Skills
- ❏ TQM/Continuous Quality Improvement

❏ **Please send me information on the topics checked above**

Name: _____

Organization: _____

Address: _____

City: _____ State: _____ Zip: _____

MAIL TO: SIGNATURE RESOURCES,
222 Milwaukee, Suite 409, Denver, CO 80206
Nationally recognized speakers are available for conference presentations.